The Greeks,
Their Heritage,
and Its Value Today

Demetrios J. Constantelos

D0167564

Hellenic College Press
Brookline, Massachusetts

Published by Hellenic College Press
50 Goddard Avenue
Brookline, Massachusetts 02146

Permission to reprint the images from Nicholas Zias,
Fotios Kontoglou, Artist (Φώτιος Κόντογλου, Ζωγράφος) is
gratefully acknowledged.

Library of Congress
Cataloging-in-Publication Data
Constantelos, Demetrios J.
The Greeks: their heritage, and its value today/Demetrios J.
Constantelos.
   p.   cm.
Includes bibliographical references and index.
ISBN 0-917653-47-5 (pbk.)
   1. Greece—Civilization. 2. National characteristics, Greek.
I. Title.
DF741.C66
949.5—dc20   96-21691
                                     CIP

For my grandchildren,
Damon, Alexander, Michael,
Peter, and Julia
in the hope that someday
they may want to learn more
about their heritage

Contents

Prologue

"The Greeks have educated Europe twice: the first time through the Parthenon, the symbol of the ancient Greek genius; and the second time through the cathedral of Hagia Sophia, the symbol of Byzantine civilization."
Gyula Moravcsik*

Byzantium and the Magyars, tr. by S. R.. Rosenbaum and M. Szegedy-Maszak. Amsterdam 1970. Page 36.
Dr. Moravcsik, an internationally known scholar, was a professor of Byzantine studies at the University of Budapest and a member of Hungary's Academy of Arts and Sciences.

Introduction

In the present essay* I highlight some of the essentials of Greek History and analyze briefly several major religious, ethical, social, and political ideas of the ancient Greeks and suggest how these ideas affect us today. In speaking of the ancient Greeks, I mean those who lived in the Mycenaean-Homeric age, the Classical, Hellenistic, Roman, and proto-Byzantine centuries. Pre-Christian and Christian Hellenism constitute a people and a culture of a recorded history of nearly four thousand years. The transition from Pagan to Christian, from antiquity to the middle ages in Greek history has been identified with the closing of the Academy of Athens in 529 by Emperor Justinian, who introduced the idea of the Christian *Oikoumene*, the belief that the ancient world had declined, transformed and renewed by Christianity.

Many important ideas of remote Greek antiquity, namely the period described by Homer, are of a diachronic nature surviving throughout antiquity and the middle ages, down to our own times. But every chronological period of ancient Greek history gave birth to some important and influential ideas. My essay therefore will be inclusive of ideas whose origins can be traced back to the Homeric age and ideas born in late antiquity, that is from the eighth century before Christ to the middle of the sixth century of our era. History is continuous and periodizations are made for practical pedagogical reasons. The uninterrupted survival of the Greek language, both oral and written, is an indication not only of the linguistic but also cultural and intellectual continuity of the Greek people.

Gyula (Julius) Moravscik, a leading European scholar of an-

1

cient and Byzantine Hellenism, writes that the Greeks have civilized Europe twice. The Parthenon on the Acropolis of Athens
stands as the symbol of the contributions of ancient Greece to
Western Civilization, and the Cathedral of Hagia Sophia in Greek
Byzantion, renamed Constantinople, present day Istanbul, stands
as the symbol of the contributions of Christian Hellenism (Byzantine) to Western Civilization. He accurately sees Hellenism holis-
tically with changes from century to century but also with uninterrupted continuity. Christianity, though heavily Hellenized, is
the one single factor which contributed to a major change and
transformation of Hellenism. But on this subject more later.

There is hardly a serious historian and student of philosophy,
religion, art, and culture in general who can minimize the importance of the ancient Greeks for Western Civilization, European,
Near Eastern, and American. Some twenty centuries ago, the Roman poet Horace wrote that "Greece, taken captive [by Rome]
captured her savage conqueror, and brought the arts to rustic
Latium (*Graecia capta ferum victorem cepit, et artis Intulit agresti
Latio*).[1] But there is no need to go back and see how the Romans
and the people of the Renaissance and early modern Europe viewed
the contributions of the ancient Greeks. One thing is certain: Nineteenth century scholars, historians, philosophers, poets were exu-
berant about our debt to the ancient Greeks. The British philosopher and poet Percy Shelley (1792-1822) writes that "we are all
Greeks. Our laws, our literature, our religion, our art, have their
root in Greece." And the German dramatist and historian Johann
von Schiller (1759-1805) went even further than Shelley when he
wrote that "everything except the blind forces of nature is of Greek
origins."[2]

Twentieth century scholarly opinion is just as enthusiastic about
the ideas, achievements, and contributions of ancient Hellenism.
I will cite only three scholars. The leading American historian of
ancient Greece, Chester G. Starr of the University of Michigan,
writes: "Why learn about the ancient Greeks?..."

One answer is clear he writes. These are the people who began
our civilization. Much of the world around us at this moment was
created only yesterday, or the day before yesterday; and we all are
the fruit of ideas, beliefs, and skills which do not change rapidly.
Our way of thought, called Western Civilization, is based on po-

litical, artistic, and intellectual principles which can be traced from modern times to medieval Europe, from medieval Europe to ancient Rome, and from Rome to Greece. Further back we cannot go, for the Greeks began it.[3] And Will Durant, the American cultural historian, author of the monumental eleven volume *Story of Civilization* and several other works, adds:

> Excepting machinery, there's hardly anything secular in our culture that does not come from Greece. Schools, gymnasiums, arithmetic, geometry, history, rhetoric, physics, biology, anatomy, hygiene, therapy, cosmetics, poetry, music, tragedy, comedy, philosophy, theology, agnosticism, skepticism, ... ethics, atheism, politics, philanthropy, tyranny, aristocracy, monarchy, democracy...these are all Greek words ... first matured for good or evil by the abounding energy of the Greeks.[4]

Durant's remarks indicate that perhaps the easiest way to understand our debt to ancient Hellenism (whether Eastern, of the Chersonese, or Western) is not to go to a museum, or to Washington and admire Greek art and architecture, but to study and analyze terms and words in the English language, or any other European language. A language is a mirror of ideas, interests, problems, occupations, names, and experiences of the people that use them. There is a strong causal relationship between the dictionary and the interests of a people. People have words for ideas, objects and experiences with which they are concerned and lack words for objects, and experiences with which they have fewer dealings. Numerous terms in the humanities, the social and physical sciences, and some 58% of the medical lexicon derive from the Greek world of ideas and experiences, an indication of their permanent influence.

In view of the overwhelming evidence, the British historian Kathleen Freeman observes that the ancient Greeks "contributed in less than a millennium more to the human treasury of civilization than all the rest of the world put together throughout all its known history." It is true however that the ancient Greeks inherited from other people some of their techniques, concepts, and motifs but whatever they inherited they transformed into something new. In the realm of ideas in particular the Greeks proved very original. No wonder therefore that expert scholars write that "from the Greeks came so many of our mental skills . . . that one could almost say that they discovered the mind"[5] and that "the rise of thinking among the Greeks was nothing less than a revolution."[6] While until several years ago all praises were bestowed upon the Greeks of the Classical Age, today we have come to appreciate the ideas, the achievements, and the contributions of the Greeks of the Hellenistic and the Roman centuries, down to the middle of the sixth century of our era, and even beyond. It is for this reason that historians consider the Parthenon in Athens and Hagia Sophia in Byzantion-Constantinople as the symbols of the two phases of the Greek impact on Western Civilization.

I consider it appropriate, therefore, and historically justifiable that we do not limit our inquiry into the main ideas of the "Golden Age" of ancient Hellenism but that we include ideas from the whole spectrum of ancient Hellenism of every geographical area—Eastern, the Continent, and Western. Ancient Hellenism was never a geographical region and Greece as we know it today emerged in recent years. The contributions we are talking about derived from Athens in the continent, but also from Miletos and Ephesos in Asia Minor; from Stageira in Thrace but also Acragas in Sicily; from Antioch in Syria and Alexandria in Egypt; from pagan Athens and Christian Byzantion.

Notes

*This essay is a slightly revised and expanded version of lectures delivered on January 5, 1990, at Taylor University, Upland, Indiana, under the title *Some Major Ideas of the Ancient Greeks and How These Ideas Affect Us Today,* and at a Symposium *On Being Greek,* sponsored by the Center for Greek Studies, Montreal, 1988.

[1] Horatius, *Epistolarum,* Bk. 2.1, 156-57.

[2] The literature on Greek influences on English literature is vast. For illustrations and discussion see J. A. K.Thomson, Cla*ssical Background of English Literature* (London Allen and Unwin, 1948), idem, *Classical Influences on English Poetry* (London: Allen and Unwin, 1951).

[3] Chester G. Starr, *The Ancient Greeks* (New York: Oxford University Press, 1971), p. 3.

[4] Will Durant, *The Life of Greece: The Story of Civilization,* part 2 (New York: Simon and Schuster, 1939), p. vii.

[5] Chester G. Starr, p. 4.

[6] Bruno Snell, *The Discovery of the Mind* (New York: Dover Publications, 1982), p. 4.

One

Names and Phases, Continuity and Change in Greek History

I

The nearly four thousand year history of Hellenism is usually divided in the following nine periods: The Minoan-Cycladic, Mycenaean, Archaic, Classical, Hellenistic, Roman, Byzantine, Ottoman, and Modern. But history knows no periods, only a continuum, and the Greek heritage has diachronic dimensions. The distinctions named above have been introduced for pedagogical and practical reasons. In reality there is a single perpetual Greek tradition. From the outset we may emphasize that there have been changes and alterations, but no discontinuity or disruptions in the evolution of the Greek heritage. Whether through linguistic, cultural, racial characteristics, or national consciousness, Hellenism has had an unbroken continuity for nearly four millennia. The term Hellenism is used here to denote both a people and a culture, a people which has been known throughout history by different names such as Hellenes, Greeks, Rhomaioi (Romans), and Yavanites (Ionians). All are synonymous and refer to the same people. Everyone of these names has its roots in history.

Hellenes is the national name for the people we call Greek. It derives from the mythical Hellene, the son of Deukalion, and father of the race. The term *Greeks* is of disputed etymology. It derives either from the people of *Graioi* of Boeotia, who first settled in Italy in the eighth century before Christ, thus the Latin form *Graeci* and the modern form Greeks; or from a tribe in Epeiros, in northwestern Greece, named *Graici-Grai-ikoi.*

5

In any case it is from the name *Graioi* that the Hellenes have become known to the Europeans as Greeks. Some ancient Greek sources such as Aristotle, Apollodoros, the Chronicle of Paros indicate that the ancient Hellenes were first called Greeks (*Graikoi*). The third name is *Yavanites*, or *Yunani*. It derives from the Greek tribe of the Ionians, who first came into contact with Semitic and other people of the Near East. It is used to the present day by Arabs, Israelis, and others. The fourth name common among the Greeks themselves, from late antiquity to the present, is *Rhomioi*. It was adopted after many Greeks became citizens of the Roman Empire, especially after AD 212 when the half Greek-Emperor Caracallus gave the franchise to all the free inhabitants of the Roman Empire. Caracallus' edict identified all the Greeks with Rome, providing the judicial foundation of the idea of Romania. Thus all the Greeks became *populi Romani*, Romans-*Rhomioi*. The names Hellenes, *Graeci* (Greeks) and *Rhomioi* have been used by the Greeks interchangeably since the middle of the fifteenth century.

The employment of four different names for the same people should not surprise us. That a self-identification may be different from an external or foreign identification is not a historical paradox. Two examples will suffice. The natives of the New World were given by the early European explorers the generic name Indians. But the natives, classified by language type, were known among themselves by different names such as Algonquins, Iroquois, Cherokees, Tuscaroras, etc. The European people who think of themselves as *Deutsch* are to us Germans, *Allemands* to the French, and *Tedeschi* to the Italians.

Hellenism includes not only a people but also a culture, including a language which has an unbroken oral tradition of more than 3500 years and a continuous written tradition of more than 2800. Parenthetically now, but more later, let us remember that three-fourths of the Homeric lexicon is alive and used today in modern Greek.

Hellenism includes values, beliefs, customs, practices, and a consciousness that holds a people together. It is because of the accumulated wealth, the weight of the past and the conflicts between the very old, the medieval, and the modern that Greek thinkers such as George Seferis have characterized the modern Greek as a *psyche* in continuous tension. But how much of modern Greek culture can trace its roots to medieval and ancient Hellenism? What unites and what disunites the "Greeks" in history? What is the basis of their unity from one era to another? Is it possible that their historical consciousness, which emphasizes an unbroken continuity, may be the result of invented traditions and a creation of the nineteenth century?

It is a well-known fact that whether for political, nationalistic, or social reasons many traditions were invented, especially in nineteenth and early twentieth century Europe. Social organizations, clubs, and ethnic minorities created traditions in the hope of ensuring a social cohesion and an identity.[1] But while there is little doubt that political leaders and officials or organizations have invented traditions and created presuppositions to serve their objectives, it is most doubtful that the common folk, rural populations, and ordinary urban people deliberately invented traditions to enhance either their national consciousness or nationalistic objectives. Public holidays, religious rituals and ceremonies, heroes and symbols honored in the daily life of the Greeks, whether in Greece proper or Greek communities in the diaspora, are not newly invented phenomena. Many of the cultural traditions and social practices of the modern Greeks can be traced step-by-step back to remote antiquity. In the study of Greek history, we do not depend on the inspiration of a memory, however great, but on the power of a presence— the presence of the heritage, the language, and indeed the people. It is this principle that sustains the belief that in the Greek tradition there has been change, even invented beliefs, but more continuity between centuries of history than discontinuity. A common Hellenism persists, linking one phase of its development with the other.

Herodotus relates that there was a rumor in fifth century Greece that the Athenians might turn their back toward fellow Hellenes and become traitors in their struggle against the Persian invader. The Athenians responded by emphasizing that even if they wanted to cooperate with the Persians, their common Hellenism with the Lacedaimonians, Arcadians, Thebans, Corinthians, and others would prevent them from such a cooperation with the Persians. This, of course, was not necessarily true because their common Hellenism did not always prevent the ancient Hellenes from fighting with each other or from making alliances with foreigners against fellow Hellenes.

However, our concern here is not the disagreement between Sparta and Athens but the definition that the Athenians provided about the Hellenes, described by Herodotus as a people "being of the same stock and the same speech, common religion, (shrines of the Gods and rituals) and similar customs."[2] Being of the same stock, speaking the same language, having the same religion and adhering to the same customs and traditions were the elements of their common identity. But did that kind of Hellenism survive the Roman conquest, the Germanic invasions, the Slavic penetration, the Ottoman rule, natural catastrophes, famines, and pestilences? To what degree could modern Hellenism claim continuity with Ottoman, Byzantine, Roman, and ancient Hellenism? How many of those elements that characterized the unity of ancient Hellenism have survived in the history and life of modern Hellenism?

It is a well-known fact that by the ninth century before Christ many significant aspects of the Mycenaean civilization had drastically declined in the Greek world. Whether through natural catastrophes or the Doric invasions, palaces and acropolises lay in ruins, and many political as well as social and economic institutions and practices disappeared.

Nevertheless, the Greeks of the archaic and the classical periods (800 B.C.–323 B.C.) had not forgotten the Mycenaean age and they were able to recognize most of its outstanding features. Furthermore they were conscious of their own continuity with them and throughout the archaic and classical age they had retained a vivid memory of the Mycenaean episodes as the various myths, religious observances, and especially writings indicate. Nevertheless, there are scholars who believe that certain major events caused discontinuity in Greek history.

In a provocative study, the classical scholar Rhys Carpenter writes of two events that caused a discontinuity in the history of Greek civilization: one occurred during the twelfth century before the Christian era and the second during the seventh century after Christ.[3] He attributes both disruptions to natural catastrophes rather than to invasions by related or foreign tribes. Whether or not we accept his thesis, the fact is that he was right in identifying those two centuries as critical in the history of Greek civilization. The first one is associated with the descent and diffusion of the Dorian Greeks, who, presumably brought the Mycenaean period to an end. However, the Doric invasion did not destroy Hellenism. In the last analysis, the Dorians themselves were Greeks. The Dorians introduced a change but not radical discontinuity. The second event is associated with the Slavic invasions of the seventh century after Christ. Whether for political reasons, personal prejudices, or foreign propaganda, the Slavic invasions have attracted more attention. But did they destroy the Greek race? Did they cause a cataclysmic discontinuity in the history of the Greek nation?

No serious and objective scholar today subscribes to the nineteenth century theory that the Slavic penetration into the Greek peninsula was so catastrophic that the Greek race disappeared from the face of the earth. Despite several important studies and recent advances in our understanding of the Slavic invasions in Greece, Slavic remains there are still rare and much disputed. Most authorities agree that, "there was no question of any permanent Slavonization of Greek territory" in the words of the Russian-Serbian historian George Ostrogorsky.[4] The Slavic invasions resulted not in the destruction of the native population but in the establishment of Slavic enclaves in the Greek chersonese. Ultimately the foreign settlements were absorbed by the indigenous population and Hellenized. They left behind only place names and affected neither the literate language nor popular religious beliefs, or the culture of the natives. Furthermore, the sources referring to Slavic penetration of the seventh century are not supported by other historical events implying that the Greeks were so overwhelmed that they could not recover themselves or continue their former way of life. The prevailing Byzantine scholarly opinion today has been summarized as follows:

> Notwithstanding the various tribes and peoples that settled on the territory of the (Byzantine) Empire....

the prevailing population was as Greek or Hellenized as it had been in the Balkans and Asia Minor during the fourth through sixth centuries (A.D.). Certainly, there were ethnic minorities there sometimes inclined to secession (the Italians, Bulgarians, Armenians, and so on), but the main ethnic substratum consisted, throughout Byzantine history, of Greek and Hellenized constituents. The language remained unchanged... Byzantium retained the diglossia, the artificial gap between the language of literature and the spoken vernacular...[5]

More serious than the arguments concerning the results of the invasions by various tribes and natural catastrophes is the view that the conversion of the Greeks to Christianity introduced a more drastic discontinuity in their history. In the last analysis, *Rhomiosini* is identified with the Christian Orthodox nature of Hellenism. Slowly but steadily, from the first to the tenth century of our era, Christianity altered many aspects of the Greek people's mentality and culture, not only religious creed and worship but also art and ritual, outlook and philosophy of history, onomatology and ethical values.

The adoption of Christianity by the Greeks, however, did not cause a discontinuity in their history but only a transformation. The relationship between the old and the new aspects of a civilization is evolutionary rather than revolutionary. Christianity, the product of Hellenistic Judaism and Hellenism proper, introduced new ideas but non-Christian and Christian Hellenism were not as antithetical as some people would like us to believe. Much of Christianity's doctrine, mind, spirit, ritual, and art is closer to Hellenic than Hebrew roots. For example, the critical spirit of ancient Hellenism was inseparable from the Christian debates of medieval Hellenism. Christian art, Byzantine iconography in particular, has deep roots in ancient Hellenism. The veneration of icons was viewed by the iconoclasts of the eighth century as a pagan custom of Hellenic origin. "Throughout the history of medieval Byzantium, whether in letters or in art or in other activities of the human spirit, it was impossible to escape from what has been called 'perennial

Hellenism"' in the words of Ernst Kitzinger, who is one of the leading art historians of the Middle Ages.

In the course of nearly ten centuries, Hellenism converted to Christianity but in the process of its conversion it Hellenized Christianity, making it an integral part of medieval and modern Greek culture. And the survival of culture is the best witness of continuity in the Greek tradition.

History reveals that empires and states may rise and fall, but cultures of a people proves more resilient than structures and governmental institutions. Nations have a way of saving the destruction of their cities and even the killing of a certain or large percentage of their population. In the course of one or two generations they are able to restore their previous cultural conditions. It is on this historical evidence that the late Arnold Toynbee writes vigorously about the continuity and the interrelationships between the various stages of the Greek heritage.[6]

As already indicated, in the history of the Greeks, there were recessions, alterations, and reformulations, but no radical disruptions. There is no more certain indication of cultural collapse and ethnic discontinuity than the failure to transmit the use of letters, the language, once this use has been acquired. Notwithstanding many foreign invasions and centuries of foreign rule, the Greek language and established ways of thinking have survived, displaying an enormous resilience. Linguistic theoreticians have demonstrated that the "belief structure" of a culture is founded upon language. Where deliberate and successive suppression of native languages has taken place, native culture has disappeared and radically altered. One's cultural and even personal identity is threatened when one's language system is threatened. From the historical view point it is more important to demonstrate linguistic relationship between one historical age and another than it is to establish racial kinship. Linguistic relationship has an intimate bearing on past cultural association while radical kinship may be quite devoid of concrete historical evidence.[7]

Language, popular or laic religion, and customs have been very consistent elements in the history of Greek culture. For example, a modern Greek with little education understands New Testament Greek better than an ordinary Englishman understands Chaucer. Even though during the later Roman and throughout the Byzantine period the Greeks were deprived of their national name because Hellenic, Hellene, and *Hellenismos* had become synonymous with paganism, their language, ethnic, and cultural consciousness were no less Greek than those of the ancient Greeks. The aesthetic and literary achievements and the political mind of ancient Hellas were admired by the Byzantine Greeks, who regarded the heritage of ancient Hellas as pagan, but nevertheless their own, an integral part of their secular education.[8]

It was respect and admiration for the past, rather than any sense of superiority over the ancients, that prompted the Byzantine Greeks to fear innovation and disruptions with the past. The Greek Christian Byzantines, like their predecessors in the pagan Roman Empire, looked upon the intellectual and literary achievements of classical Greece as the highest productions of their kind. But the intellectual products of pagan Hellenism were viewed as subordinate and propaideutic to Christian teaching, rather than as the sum of human knowledge, as they had been considered in pre-Christian times.

Under the weight of the past, the medieval Greek emphasis was on preservation, commentary, study, and imitation. With a few exceptions, Byzantine *paideia* was *paideia* through imitation rather than search, inquiry, and discovery. Thus, admiration of the classical patrimony prevented innovation and discontinuity. Fear that neoterisms might disrupt their continuity with the past controlled the human impulse to break through and achieve drastic changes, even though medieval Greek civilization was never static for it possessed its own dynamics and possessed its own integrity.

In addition to their attachment to their classical heritage, the Byzantines were fearful of innovations on account of Christianity's absolute claims. Christianity emphasized that it possessed the full and final revelation of the truth; thus it impeded the intellectual quest of the Greek Christian mind, which was not encouraged to search for new horizons and intellectual pursuits—save for certain areas, such as religious art and poetry. Indeed it was the Christian religion that introduced more change and discontinuity with ancient Hellenism. But, in the last analysis, Christianity did not disrupt but only transformed Hellenism, and that only in part. There is little doubt that Christianity had absorbed much of the ethos of ancient Hellenism— its philosophy, language, social, and family values. History confirms that the nature of a people is reflected in their human values, their emotions, their attitudes, and other elements which have remained constants in human nature. The intellectual ethos, the thought and culture of a people, is rooted in and conditioned primarily by their language.

Linguists and anthropologists, as well as psychologists, literary critics, and sociologists, have emphasized that language is the supreme evidence not only of the survival but also of the character and psyche of a people. A people's perception of the cosmos and their ways of thinking about it are profoundly influenced by the structure of the language they speak. The structure of a language and its lexicon not only determine the manner in which we understand the environment but also reflect our cultural milieu. A language sustains ethnic character as well as inhibits a people from seeing other cultures and other realities.

The morphology of a language and the content of its lexicon affect the mind and thereby much of the thought, the culture, and the outlook upon life of a given people. The language of a community or a nation directly reflects its physical, social, cultural, and ethnic physiognomy and character. The lexicon of a language is a complex inventory of ideas, interests, and occupations that take up the attention of the community. Differences between the grammars of different languages correspond not merely to differences in modes of thought but to differences in cultures as well. The survival of the Greek language is the greatest evidence of continuity in the history of Hellenism.[9]

In the Byzantine Empire, minorities were known by their ethnic names—Armenian, Bulgarian, Jewish, Slavic. Their descendants had identified themselves with Greek culture, they spoke Greek as their native tongue, and, if they were educated, their secular education was based on the Greek literary and intellectual heritage. Thus the only difference between a Byzantine Greek and a Byzantine Jew was in religion.[10] All subjects considered themselves integral elements of the Byzantine state, which they viewed as their home and their country. Language and education were decisive factors in the formation of their national identity and their state's ethnic character. It is important to observe that Armenians, Russians, Franks, Venetians, Spaniards, Germans, Khazars, and Jews of the diaspora called the subjects of the Byzantine Empire "Greeks" and the Empire itself "Greece." Hebrew inscriptions of Khazaria speak of the whole Empire, including the Balkan peninsula and Asia Minor, as "Greece" and its inhabitants as "Greeks."[11]

There are many other examples; the following will suffice. An eleventh century Armenian historian writes of the Armenians in the service of the "Greek Empire." The Syrian monk Joshua the Stylite writes about the "Greek soldiers" who assisted the sick of Edessa in a famine of the sixth century; in the seventh century Pseudo-Methodios writes of the "rulers of the Greeks, that is the Romans." Bishop Liudprand of Cremona in the tenth century complains about the attitude of the "Greeks," and the German Emperor Frederick II addressed letters to the "*Basileus* of the Greeks." The eleventh century Russian Primary Chronicle constantly refers to the "Byzantines" as Greeks, and for the Russians, Greece was the Byzantine Empire.[12]

As in Greek antiquity, when a Greek was identified with his city or home and referred to as an Athenian, a Spartan, Messinian, Samian, Arcadian, and so on, likewise in the medieval Greek Empire the identification of a person with his city, province, or eparchy of birth was very common. Thus the sources speak of *Irene e Athenaia, Theodoros o Tebaios, Phokas o Kappadokis, Vasileios o Makedon, Loukios o Makedon, Loukios o Alexandreus, Ioustinos o Thrax,* etc. Of course when a specific context warranted it, a person would call himself a Roman, a subject of the Roman Empire, which for the Byzantines had not perished with the decline and fall of the old Rome. In addition, as the ancient Persians, Romans, Egyptians, and others called the Athenians, Spartans, and citizens of other city-states of the ancient Greek World not by their city name but collectively as Greeks, likewise most of the neighbors of the Byzantine Empire and other foreign nations designated its subjects as Greeks. As we indicated earlier, the difference between self-identification and the identification by others as we observe it in the history of ancient, medieval, and modern Hellenism is neither a paradox nor a unique phenomenon for it is common in many societies and on several levels.[13]

The notion that language is a fundamental element of ethnicity and of cultural identity, as contemporary linguistics has emphasized, was not a strange one to the Byzantines. Some of their intellectuals echoed this very "modern" theory. Nikephoros Choumnos urged his contemporary writers to imitate and remain faithful to the purity and clarity of ancient Greek as befits Greeks; Pletho Gemistos defined the ethnicity of his compatriots on the basis of the language they spoke and their *paideia* (education, culture).[14]

The very attachment to ancient Greek, as well as the numerous admonitions of Byzantine intellectuals and writers concerning its cultivation and the preservation of its purity, is strong evidence that the Byzantines had no doubts about their links with ancient Hellas. "For them it was unthinkable to express their minds and their feelings in a language other than ancient Greek," in the words of Professor E. Kriaras, who reminds us that *diglossia,* too, was a problem in the Byzantine era as it had been in modern Hellenism.[15] To depart from the ancient language was a neoterism, a departure from the right rules introduced by their Greek ancestors.

Furthermore, the persistence of archaic forms of language and the emphasis on ancient Greek, Attic in particular, indicate that Byzantine society was very slow in making changes. A growing society usually develops changes in its language, as reflected in its lexicon, semantics, syntax, grammar, and other elements. Language, as well as religious beliefs, popular religiosity in particular, and the intellectual heritage of a given nation at a given time are relative to the whole mental attitude of that time. In the language, the culture, and the philosophical outlook of the Greeks neither abrupt nor permanent changes have taken place. Language shapes culture and culture shapes language. There is a constant interaction between the two. The language and the mind of modern Greeks and the Byzantines are in a direct continuity with those of the Hellenic past.

Several leading specialists have demonstrated "through the

facts, both historical and linguistic, that the long tradition of
the Greek language through centuries and millennia since earliest recorded antiquity was, in fact never broken but sustained
for 3,350 years since Mycenaean Greek began to be recorded..."
in the words of an outstanding linguist and philologist.[16] Continuity in the history of the Greek language is closely related
to the continuity of Greek culture and the Greek people. Other
scholars see the continuity of the Greek nation in its epic poetry, lamentations, popular religious festivals in honor of saints,
and popular heroes.

In Byzantium traditions were usually inherited. As elements
of social life, religious practices, customs, institutions, speech,
dress, laws, songs, and tales, the survival of traditions was determined by repetition which automatically implies continuity
with the past. Repetition is in harmony with the human nature which has remained consistent throughout the ages of
human history. Human nature is conditioned by the values and
morals of family and society, religious values in particular which
tend to remain habitual among people everywhere.

Many elements which can be observed in Byzantine social
and religious life were of the Hellenistic period, tracing their
roots back to the classical age. Culturally a "Byzantine" was a
person of Hellenic speech and Hellenic education based on the
great classics of ancient Hellenism. And religion included not
only Christian scriptures and sublime Christian theology and
liturgy, but also religious festivals and practices whose origins
have been traced to ancient Hellas.[17]

In the culture of the modern Greeks, the descendants of the
Byzantine Greeks, in their psychology, their literature, their
religious beliefs and practices, and above all their consciousness there exists a permanent substratum which layer by layer
can be traced back to the Byzantine, Roman, Hellenistic, the
Classical, and even remote antiquity.

There is little doubt while many traditions were inherited
others were "invented," on the basis of new experiences and
new influences especially those related to Christian beliefs,
church rituals, and practices. Nevertheless, it was rather un-
common to find theologians and churchmen who exerted conscious efforts to achieve a break with the past, its culture, lan-

guage, philosophy, and social ethos. On the other hand there were intellectuals who made calculated efforts to maintain, or re-establish continuity with, the historic past through a revival of practices, methods, rules, and especially the language of the past.

In the area of language and literature a striking example comes from the attitude of the Christian intellectuals of the early centuries of our era. As early as the second century the *koine* Greek, the language of the Greek translation of the Hebrew Bible (Septuagint) and the New Testament, was abandoned by the early Christian writers. Even though it carried the authority of "the word of God," Christian intellectuals including the Apologists (Justin), the Apostolic Fathers (Irenaios), and later the Alexandrians (Clement, Origen, Athanasios, Kyrillos), the Antiochians (John Chrysostom, Theodore of Mopsuestia, Theodoret of Cyrus), and the Cappadocians (Basil of Caesarea, Gregory of Nyssa, Gregory the Theologian, of Nazianzus), returned to the language of the classical Greek writers thus establishing a continuity with the literate ancient Greek world. In the area of historiography, once again the language of Eusebius of Caesarea in the fourth century, Prokopios in the sixth century, Anna Comnena in the twelfth, and John Kantakouzenos in the fourteenth, was not simply a calculated imitation or apeing of Thucydides but a conscious or subconscious effort to re-establish a link with the "pagan"—their own cultural and intellectual heritage.[18]

The same phenomenon can be discerned in other areas of linguistic expression such as medicine. Following the example of Galen, Byzantine medical authors intentionally used the Attic language of ancient Greek medical authors. It is beyond the scope of this essay to establish the continuity between Byzantine literature and ancient Greek literature, a topic which has been discussed for many years by competent philologists.

One of the major links between ancient and medieval Hellenism is in the sphere of popular religiosity.

II

The tenacity with which ancient Greek religious beliefs, rituals and customs survived in the medieval Greek, or Byzantine world, is astonishing. Notwithstanding many foreign invasions, old religious beliefs and lower forms of religion that can trace their origin to the ancient Greek world persist in the popular imagination of the medieval as well as modern Greek.[19]

How do we explain this religious and cultural continuity with the past? Did ancient Greek religious practices survive through Byzantium and modern Greece because of the effort of the educated classes, who took a keen interest in their literary, religious, and esthetic value? Is the presence of so many old traditions in modern Greece the result of a revival or simply a natural *survival*?

While it is possible that in certain cases the educated classes with their knowledge of ancient Greek literature, religion, myth, and traditions influenced the popular imagination, it seems very improbable that ancient Greek religiosity has defied time and persists even today because of determined efforts to keep it alive. There were a number of elements of ancient Greek religious practices which entered into early and medieval Christianity and became integral parts of Byzantine and neo-Hellenic religion. For example, in ancient Greece a statue became an object of worship only at the moment or after its consecration; in the Byzantine era an icon is venerated only after its consecration, a tradition that has survived to the present day; in ancient Greece a votive or *vota* representing the parts of the body healed were offered to temples and statues; offering votive or vota representing parts of the body healed by a miraculous icon to icons is a common practice in Greek towns and villages; belief in ancient Greece that only certain statues such as the Pallas Athena or Apollo of Magnesia had miraculous powers continued to be practiced in Byzantium; only certain icons, such as the icon of Zoodochos Peghe, were believed to have miraculous powers; Greek *choreia* were transformed into Byzantine *threnoi,* or lamentations; the ancient Greeks called Asclepios *Philanthropos Soter* as the medieval Greeks described Christ as the *Philanthropos Soter;* the ancient Greeks built hospitals or clinics next to temples and Byzantine hospitals were erected next to churches; incubation, i.e., sleeping in a consecrated part of a temple for healing purposes or for divine dreams was common practice in the ancient Greek world; sleeping in the church for healing purposes so that Christ, His mother the *Theotokos* or saints may appear in dreams is being practiced to the present day in the Greek World; belief in demonology and exorcism were common in ancient Greece as they are common in today.

The institutionalized medieval Greek Church condemned many gross superstitions, such as enchanters and amulet givers, the calends, and fortune tellers,[20] but with little success. But neither the Byzantine Church nor the state apologized for the survival of the past, its life and culture. In the last analysis, they viewed the Christian synthesis not as a corruption but as an enrichment. The edifice of the new religious culture had plenty of space for activities, feelings, and beliefs that antedated the Christian era.

The Church did not seek separation from the old culture but pursued its consecration on a selective basis. After all, the old culture too was part of God's creation. Old beliefs and practices not only outlived legislations and canons, but they were institutionalized as well. Thus in the Byzantine era, history continued as it had been before. New cults, heresies, and creeds emerged in the Byzantine millennium, but the old held on tenaciously. The new religious, social, and political conditions that came to prevail after the age of Constantine the Great did not swallow up the old culture. In matters of healing and death, crisis and mystery, superstition and religiosity the presence of the past was very real, surviving to the present day in many rural areas of modern Greece.[21]

Many popular beliefs that now exist in Greece are in fact direct survivals from antiquity. In a recent exhaustive study, Richard Blum and Eva Blum maintain that "rural folk (in modern Greece) have experienced these life crises and mysteries under relatively unchanged conditions for the last several thousand years."[22] There are certain "constants" in human experience and human nature. The question is: how do we explain this laic religious *continuum*? What indeed has so tenaciously sustained numerous religious beliefs and practices whose roots can be traced back to the pre-Christian era? Collectively those practices constituted a stream of religious tradition and culture which defied the edicts of Theodosios and Justinian, the canons of the Church, and the condemnations of the higher clergy, and continued to flow forward peacefully and patiently irrigating many aspects of the common people's daily life. Edwin Rhode, in a profound study on the encounter between Greek thought, both philosophical and religious, with Christianity, writes: "Much—only too much—of the philosophy of its (Greece's) old age lived on in the speculative system of the Christian faith. And in the whole of modern culture so far as it has built itself upon Christianity or by extension from it, in all modern science and art, not a little survives of Greek genius and Greek inspiration... Nothing that has once been alive in the spiritual life of man can ever perish entirely; it has achieved a new form of existence in the consciousness of mankind—an immorality of its own."[23]

Religiosity, whether pagan or Christian, is part of a society's culture which reflects that society's continuous existence. Culture is dynamic and in its movement forward it carries with it its components and its characteristics. Its adaptation to new circumstances is not hindered by the emergence of new elements and events. It is a process always going on—not in stages of disruption. In the encounter between a foreign culture and an enchoric one, it is the indigenous that ultimately prevails, even though it may in its process emerge altered and reformed. Threatened by the alien, the native religion, customs, language, and traditions react in self-defense and ultimately work out the acculturation and assimilation of the foreign. When two dynamics are in conflict one or the other is destined to conquer the other, or the two are bound to blend into a new synthesis. Usually, it is the autochthonal, the native that displays more strength, more stamina, and resistance to change. The extraneous, which has already exposed itself to innovation and change and has gone through some adaptations, becomes subject to the indigenous culture and goes through even more transformations.

While Greek religiosity resisted the penetration of Christianity, in its efforts to prevail, Christianity accommodated itself to the existing cultural and religious realities. Thus ancient Greek religiosity as the native dynamic, resisted the advance of the new religion and in their struggle a new, Byzantine Christian religiosity was born.

Furthermore every religious culture is rooted in and conditioned by a language. As we have emphasized, both language and culture are basic sources for all civilizations and major factors in the formation of a nation's physiognomy. They both recondition high and low forms of religion, rational and irrational beliefs and practices. Thus Byzantine society, with its roots in Greek and Hellenized culture, became the beneficiary as well as the conditioner of the Greek language and of Greek culture in general.

But there are additional grounds for the explanation of this continuity. The continuous existence of peasant customs, rituals, myths and a synthesis of other cultural elements have become an integral part of the Greek *psyche*. This synthesis finds legitimation as tradition by proving itself a formative force of continuity from one phase of Greek history to the other, securing the solidarity and identity of the Greeks as a group. All these elements serve as a communication and social imprinting in their life.[24] Thus immersed in those inherited ideas and practices, the native Greeks of the Byzantine Empire became instruments of transmission of old religious beliefs and practices, notwithstanding rules and regulations, exhortations, and threats against them.

Popular religion includes elements that have remained constants in human nature. Religiosity, as a popular expression of religious feelings and emotions, reveals how much of the past had survived the test of time in the Byzantine era. In the ancient as well as in the medieval periods of Greek history there were at least two distinct cultures, one peasant and one urban and elite. Medieval peasant culture had more in common with ancient peasant culture than with the contemporary Christian culture of the educated urban elite. Lower forms of religious beliefs and practices, superstitions, and occult practices were more suited to the peasant culture of both societies, ancient and medieval. The term pagan derives from this very notion. A *paganus* (pagan) was a peasant, a conservative rustic reluctant to convert to Christianity.

Furthermore, we can enlist the assistance of genetics in order that in a genetic-like transmission non-genetic phenomena may be explained. According to genetics, identifiable and inheritable characteristics of an organism that contribute to the organism's potential for survival are sustained through continued generations of that given organism. Those characteristics which are either noncontributory or anti-survival, since they lessen the individual organism's potential for survival, are lost from the cumulative genetic pool and withdrawn to a relatively recessive state.

Many identifiable nonphysical phenomena, such as religiosity, and hero and martyr worship that are parts of the overall behavioral pattern of an individual, of a group of individuals, of cultural, ethnic, or religious societies that help in any way to provide an increased potential gratification of some basic drive of the entity involved, emerge as dominant characteristics, and as such they survive and are propagated. The propagation of such phenomena may be completely unconscious on the part of the people involved or it may be the result of a very deliberate and organized effort.

Medieval Greek society after Julian the Apostate's reign did not exert any deliberate and organized efforts to preserve ancient Greek paganism. The contrary is true. Imperial legislation and Church canons repeatedly condemned paganism. Greek paganism was propagated unconsciously by the enchoric people who viewed the infiltration of the new as a threat to their own survival. Biologically speaking, the most universally constant survival characteristic of an organism lies in its ability to adapt to changing environments. Non-biological phenomena such as ancient beliefs and practices, have survived in many forms because of the ability of their transmitters to adapt to new circumstances.

In addition to the evidence of language and popular religion, the survival of the race itself needs to be emphasized. Leading physical anthropologists find more homogeneity between modern Greeks and their very remote ancestors than between modern Western Europeans and their ancestors. Professor Carleton Stevens Coon of Harvard writes: "It is inaccurate to say that the modern Greeks are different physically from the ancient Greeks. Such a statement is based on an ignorance of the Greek ethnic character." Coon finds more affinity between the Greeks of the sixth century before Christ and modern Greeks than between the Germans described by Tacitus and modern South Germans. He concludes his observations on the Greek race with these remarks: "It is my personal reaction to the living Greeks that their continuity with their ancestors of the ancient world is remarkable, rather than opposite."[25]

The Greek anthropologist Ares Poulianos, trained in the Soviet Union, who might have had reason to stress the old theory that the modern Greeks are Hellenized Slavs, a theory that was propagandized by Greek Marxists in the 1940s, has reached the same conclusions as Coon. Dr. Poulianos cites several prominent anthropologists of the Soviet Union who acknowledge the continuity of Greek culture and believe in the survival of the Greeks as a race.[26] The Danish-British scholar John Geipel has summarized the views of several contemporary physical anthropologists as follows: "Considering the number of incursions, of Phoenicians, Romans, Celts, Goths, Slavs, Vlachs, Turks and others, that have penetrated Greece during the past two thousand years, it is remarkable that the most conspicuous physical traits displayed by the living population of this exposed and accessible little country are probably those that were ancient hereabouts at the time of the Trojan War, let alone in Alexander's day."[27]

Several family and social values among the Greeks have their roots in remote antiquity and serve as links between centuries of Greek culture, in particular the value of *philanthropia*, or to love the human being, which is the basis of *philoxenia* (hospitality). A reading of Plutarch's *Kimon*, Diodoros Sikeliotis' account of Tellias, the lives of John the *Eleimon* and Philaretos of Pontos of the Byzantine era,[28] will convince us of the continuity of *philanthropia* as a social virtue of the Hellenes. Some of the best illustrations of Greek *philanthropia* in theory and practice in modern Greece are provided by Nikos Kazantzakis. In his *Report to Greco*, Kazantzakis writes of his grandfather in Crete, "who took his lantern each evening and made the rounds of the village to see if any stranger had come. He would take him home, feed him, give him a bed for the night, and then in the morning see him off with a cup of wine and slice of bread." In his wide travels around the world, Kazantzakis had not found similar phenomena. Not only in Crete but also in many parts of Greece the "stranger is still the unknown god," he writes.[29] Kazantzakis' accounts recall very similar examples of the Byzantine era.[30]

Language and literature, values of social and family life, religious practices, racial characteristics, customs, institutions, songs, tales, and festivities that can be traced back to remote antiquity, have endured foreign invasions and years of enslavement and have survived to the present day because their bearers have survived. Some of these principles have found support among Americans of Greek origin.

Dr. Alice Scourby, the author of a recent thesis on values and attitudes of Greek Americans, reveals that third-generation Americans of Greek descent were found to favor the persistence of ethnic values and expressed strong sentiments of attachment to the sub-community, that is the Greek-Orthodox community within the American society at large, a persistence that perpetuates and promotes continuity. As in antiquity and medieval and modern Hellenism, Dr. Scourby finds more continuity than discontinuity in attitudes toward religious, social, and ethnic values among Greek Americans. Language, religious, and ethnic factors are inseparable for them.[31]

In brief much evidence indicates that in the history of Hellenism and its culture in particular, there exists a permanent substratum that can be traced back through the Ottoman, the Byzantine, the Roman, the Classical, the Mycenaean, and even more remote antiquity. To be sure, Hellenism has altered, changed, and been renewed in all periods. Greek history is like a river, the mainstream rolling on despite infusion of new sources or draining off of various rivulets, or like Jason's Argo, continually refitted and refurbished over centuries so that it was all new and yet still the same Argo.

Notes

[1] See Eric Hobsbawm, "Mass-Producing Traditions: Europe 1870-1914," in Eric Hobsbawm and Terence Ranger, Editors, *The Invention of Tradition* (Cambirdge, 1983), 263-307; also Hobsbawm's introduction, 1-14.

[2] Herodotos, *Historia,* 8:144.

[3] Rhys Carpenter, *Discontinuity in Greek Civilizaton* (New York, N.Y., 1968).

[4] George Ostrogorsky, *History of the Byzantine State*, tr. Joan Hussey, Revised Edition (New Brunswick, N.J., 1969), 94.

[5] Alexander Kazhdan and Anthony Cutler, "Continuity and Discontinuity in Byzantine History" *Byzantion* vol. 52 (1982), 465.

[6] Arnold Toynbee, *The Greeks and Their Heritage* (Oxford, 1981), esp. 268-70.

[7] William Foxwell Albright, *From the Stone Age to Christianity*, 2nd ed. (New York, N.Y., 1957), 44.

[8] Granvilte Downey, "The Byzantine Church and the Presentness of the Past," *Theology Today*, 15.1 (1958), 93-4.

[9] cf. Demetrius J. Georgacas, *A Greco-Slavic Controversial Problem Re-examined...* (Athens, 1982), 195; Robert Browning, *Medieval and Modem Greek* (London, 1969).

[10] Andrew Sharf, *Byzantine Jewry* (New York, N.Y., 1971), 74, 116.

[11] Norma Golb and Omeljan Pritsak, *Khazarian Hebrew Documents of the Tenth Century* (Ithaca, 1982), 111; D.M. Dunlop, *History of the Jewish Khazars* (Princeton, 1954), 89.

[12] For references in the original sources see my article "Canon 62 of the Synod in Trullo and the Slavic Problem," *Byzantina*, 2 (Thessaloniki, 1970), 34, n. 26. Also S. Frankling "Byzantine Empire and Kievan Russia," *Byzantion*, 53.2 (1983), 507-37, esp. 526.

[13] Brian Silver, "Bilingualism and Maintenance of the Mother Tongue in Soviet Central Asia," *Slavic Review*, 35,3 (1976) 406-07.

[14] J.F. Boissonade, *Anecdota Graeca*, vol. 3 (Paris, 1833), 359; S. Lambros, *Palaiologia kai Peloponnesiaka*, vol. 3 (Athens, 1926), 247.

[15] E. Kriaras, "E Diglossia sta Ysterobyzantina Gramata," *Byzantina*, 8 (Thessaloniki, 1976), 221.

[16] Georgacas, op.cit. 195.

[17] M. Alexiou, *The Ritual Lament in Greek Tradition* (Cambridge, 1974), 187-189, 195-197. See also George Thomson, "The Continuity of Hellenism," Greece and Rome, second series, 18.1 (1971), 18-29.

[18] N.G. Wilson, *Scholars of Byzantium* (Baltimore, Md., 1983), R. Browning, "Byzantine Scholarship," *Past and Present*, 28 (1964), 3-20.

[19] See my article, "Byzantine Religiosity and Ancient Greek Religiosity," in *The 'Past' in Medieval and Modern Greek Culture*, ed. Speros Vryonis, Jr. (Malibu, Calif., 1978), 135-51.

[20] G.A. Rhalles and M. Potles, *Syntagma ton theion kai hieron kononon*, vol. 2 (Athens, 1852), 448. For an analysis see my article, "Canon 62..." op.cit.

[21] See my article, "Byzantine Religiosity..." op.cit., 146-47.

[22] Richard and Eva Blum, *The Dangerous Hour - The Lore of Crisis and Mystery in Rural Greece* (New York, N.Y., 1920), 263-64.

[23] Edwin Rhode, Psyche, *The Cult of Souls and Belief in Immortality Among the Greeks* (Freeport, N.Y., 1972, reprinted from the 1920 edition), 548-49.

[24] Here, as elsewhere in the present essay, I restate what I have written in "Byzantine Religiosity and Ancient Greek Religiosity" op.cit., esp. 146-47.

[25] Carlton Stevens Coon, *The Races of Europe* (New York, 1939), 604 607. See also Speros Vryonis, "Recent Scholarship on Continuity and Discontinuity of Culture," in *The 'Past' in Medieval and Modern Greek Culture*, op.cit., esp. 248-49.

[26] Ares N. Poulianos, *E Proeleuse ton Hellenon* (Athens, 1968), esp. 16-22, 281-83.

[27] John Geipel, *The Europeans* (New York, 1970), 216-17.

[28] For references and other illustrations on the subject see my *Byzantine Philanthropy and Social Welfare*, 2nd edition (New Rochelle, New York, 1991), chs. 1, 9.

[29] Nikos Kazantzakis, *Anafora ston Greko,* 3d ed. (Athens, 1965), esp. 373-75.

[30] See my book *Byzantine Philanthropy and Social Welfare*, 2nd edition, p. 105-111.

[31] Alice Scourby, "Three Generations of Greek Americans: A Study in Ethnicity" in the *Greek-American Community in Transition*, ed. Harry J. Psomiades and Alice Scourby (New York, 1982), 111-21.

Two

Greek Ideas and Practices of Modern and Universal Value

I

The first of the twelve main ideas I will analyze is spirituality and religious thought. From the outset I should emphasize that I am concerned here with the official trend in ancient Greek thought and not with popular religious life. While many persons know of the importance of Greek art, Greek poetry, Greek philosophy, and other aspects of ancient Greek civilization few realize that Greek religion too repays our study at the present day. The terms theology, enthusiasm, psyche, demon, ecstasy, mystery, theism, atheism, hagiology, hierarchy, and therapy derive from the Greek religious language and experience. A language learned from childhood and transmitted from generation to generation leaves its imprint upon human experience. Ancient Greek religious thought affects us today because it has put its stamp on Christian theology and practice.

One of the distinct characteristics of the evolution of Greek culture is that the lower and more embryonic forms of ideas, whether religious or philosophical, have survived through the ages either by the side or within the higher and more developed. Modern man of the Western heritage, whether a practicing Christian or not, has been nourished on a tradition in which Hebrew monotheism, reformed by Jesus Christ and Paul of Tarsus, is combined with a metaphysical theology derived from Greek philosophers—Parmenides, Plato, and Aristotle. Let us remember that Christianity, Orthodox, Catholic, Episcopal, Baptist, Evangelical, Methodist, Presbyterian, Church, Ecclesiastical, Synagogue, Pope, Patriarch, presbyter, and deacon

27

are terms of Greek origin and transmit Greek ideas, concepts, and experiences. Of course it is easier to write a history of ideas than a history of their application; the history of a religion than a history of its practice; the history of the democratic idea than a history of democracy in action.

The ancient Greeks advised: *panti theon aition ypertithemen* that is, set god over all as cause.[1] Thus the first idea we need to explore is the idea of divinity, god. But what did the ancient Greeks mean by god? What was their idea about divinity? The Greeks provided no specific definition of divinity. Whatever is immortal, is divine; whatever is divine is immortal. Divinity, deity, or god meant not a person but something alive, active, imperishable—energy. Of course one may immediately react and remind us of the Olympian gods and goddesses, and other lesser divinities of Greek mythology. Even though myths and mythology belong to the field of literature rather than religion, we need to underline that even in mythology Greek religion is neither uniform nor strictly defined. Belief in many gods and practices of cultic rites were never absent from popular religion of many ancient (Babylonian, Egyptian, Hittite, Hebrew) and modern people, including the Greeks. But many ancient Greeks interpreted their myths and mythological divinities allegorically. From as early as Minoan and Mycenaean religious myths in the Cyclades, Crete, and mainland Greece several names of goddesses appear as diverse epithets of the same divinity or diversified forms of the same entity. And lesser gods, such as Hyakinthos, appear in assimilation with the chief of gods—Zeus. Gods and goddesses have been described as a "dual monotheism." It is doubtful whether Homer himself believed in the real existence of the Olympian deities. Homer and Hesiod were accused by ancient Greeks such as Theagenes, Hekataios, Xenophanes, and Protagoras as the inventors of Greek polytheism. Whatever the case, myths and mythological divinities as emblematic of truths, whether as natural forces or human attributes, were never absent from ancient Greek thought.[2] In the last analysis archaic Greek religion recognized many divine powers in one divine cosmos.

The search for the *Arche*, the prime cause/mover, became a major concern of the ancient Greeks after the seventh century.

Divinity was the source of knowledge because it was perceived as the cause of creation of everything. "Human nature has no knowledge, but the divine nature has," said Herakleitos,[3] a belief repeated by many Greek thinkers from Homer to Aristotle. "Begin with god" is an ancient maxim which has survived and is practiced by the modern Greeks.

The idea of divinity went through stages of development, and religion among the ancient Greeks was a constant quest. The fourth century poet and philosopher Menander captured the idea of religion in ancient Greece in the following lines:

> By each of us there stands directly from birth a kind
> of mystagogic spirit to lead us through the labyrin-
> thine mysteries of life
> And we must never think this spirit evil,
> Nor fraught with wickedness to harm our lives,
> But always hold God good in everything,
> Those who themselves turn base in character and
> complicate their lives exceedingly,
> When they have ruined all through carelessness,
> Declare and hold as cause this spirit-guide,
> And make him evil, becoming such themselves.[4]

The idea of divinity not as an exclusive possession, like the god of ancient Israel, but as a universal, all-encompassing being became a central idea of the ancient Greeks. In Homeric times it was acknowledged that "all people have need of the gods—divinity."[5] The Greeks searched for the divinity in the beauty and harmony of the cosmos, the powers and forces of nature, in the logic and conscience of the human being. Thus in ancient Greek religion, the divinity is everywhere—it is a cosmic being expressed in various ways and manners. Zeus, Apollo, Athena, Demeter are names of the same divinity in different actions and as different attributes of the human being. The presence of the divinity everywhere implies the deification of the world. The unity of human nature is achieved through its unity with the *Pneuma* (Spirit) common to all human beings. The spirituality of one person can progress in relationship with the spirituality of other people in a community, like the ancient Greek polis or the Christian ecclesia (or church). Spiritual and religious duties are realized within the community and spiritual, religious, and political functions are interwoven.

The idea of divinity became subject to evolution and refinement after the sixth century. The ideas of Thales of Miletos, the first among the Greek philosophers, about divinity and the cosmos influenced later thinkers including Plato and Aristotle. Thales emphasized the spiritual nature of the cosmos, the ever-presence of the divinity everywhere and in everything. "All things are full of god" he taught. "The whole world is a living organism, filled with souls, and god is the mind behind the cosmos."[6] Later thinkers such as Plato emphasized the interrelationship between the physical and the metaphysical. Nature is neither material nor metaphysical; it is an organic whole. And the human being is a part of the whole landscape—an organic whole of the physical and the metaphysical.

From a religion of polytheism, to religious syncretism, through a belief in philosophical monotheism, the Greeks arrived at the belief in an "unknown God," who ultimately was identified with the Logos of the Gospel of John—Jesus the Christ. Their understanding of the Christian God's nature and attributes, God's relationship with the cosmos, Christian theology of the first five centuries in particular was Greek. The so-called Gentile Christianity and the Christian Church of the first five centuries was likewise Greek. In the times of Jesus and later, Gentile corresponded to Greek (Jn 7.35; Rom 3.9, etc.). Gentile stood for the culture and the religion of the Greeks and those influenced by the Greeks.

As a historical religion, Christianity was born in a Hellenistic Judaism and it quickly spread in the Greek world of late antiquity. The Christian scriptures were written entirely in Greek and Greek cities such as Antioch, Ephesus, Philippi, Thessaloniki, and Corinth were the first to be evangelized and receive Christianity. Latin Christianity was an offshoot of Greek Christianity, like a branch which grows from a tree trunk. The early Church was implanted in the Greek-speaking world and expressed itself in the Greek language for many centuries.

The idea of divinity, then, as it evolved in Greek thought, both non-Christian and Christian, is imbedded in contemporary theology which emphasizes the importance of the mystery, incomprehensibility, and God's all-encompassing love. "God is called *philios* and *etaireios*, God of love and fellowship, because God brings mankind into union, and desires that all should be friends one with another" in the words of the first century philosopher Dio Chrysostom.[7] The idea of the divinity is closely related with the idea of humanity, what it means to be human.

II

The second major idea I intend to touch upon is the idea about the human being, the *anthropos*. "There are many wonderful things, but none more wonderful than man" exclaims Sophocles' chorus in the Antigone.[8] The human person was perceived as a being having its existence in the First Being, the source of everything and present everywhere. Divinity and humanity are two powers in constant interaction and cooperation. The major contributions of the ancient Greeks to Western Civilization are based on the conception they had of the human person's ontology—the human person as a spiritual, rational (logical), moral, social, artistic, and creative evolutionary being of infinite value. Human energy was perceived as an innate divine quality, a manifestation of the Creator's vital energy. The human being represents so to speak the Supreme Being on earth. But the human was understood as a mortal destined for immortality. Only divinity is by itself immortal. The human being is a dependent being and any attempt to ignore or supersede the divinity results in severe consequences.

The two protagonists in the Homeric epics, the *Iliad* and the *Odyssey*, represent some of the central ideas of pre-classical Greece. The example of Achilles was used to teach that irrational wrath is futile and destructive, and that self-control is indispensable and a source of rewards. No matter how powerful and how clever, whether an Achilles, Agamemnon, or Odysseus, man is not god, an all-powerful being. Pride which would attempt to elevate the human to a divine status was a *hubris*, an arrogant insult against divinity, and destructive. Laws, whether of the universe, nature, or the state need to be obeyed because all laws are of divine origins.

Man must be himself and play the part he has been assigned to by nature with a sense of humility. The self, which is absent from the Old Testament, is an independent and a dependent entity and it appears balanced and measured. In the Homeric epics we discern a synergy between Divinity and humanity—the principles of religious humanism. In the Odyssey we find the ideal which should be pursued by the human mind in cooperation with the divinity. When Odysseus found himself in a hopeless situation, the divinity in the form of Ino (Leukothea) appeared and urged him not to despair but to move on, assuring him of her help.[9]

Odysseus is the prototype of the man who thinks but who also needs divine assistance. Mind and body are good in themselves and need to be in constant cooperation and harmony. The body must possess valor, endurance, health; the mind must provide intelligence, alertness, ability to function with decision-making and moderation qualities. Presence of mind and inner strength were highly admired in ancient Greece. The human mind, however, should be able to solve not only personal but also universal problems. Man by himself is not the measure of all things, but with supernatural assistance he is. Are these ideas not of contemporary value? Who doubts that these principles cannot affect our lives for the better?

Notwithstanding their understanding of man's limitations, the ancient Greeks advised: "strive always after excellence" (*aien aristeuein*),[10] using an alert mind and pursuing it through vigorous action. The idea of excellence implied an appreciation of creative intelligence, tireless inquiry, education for the sake of a good life—all harmonized and balanced. *Miden* a*gan, pan metron ariston*, nothing in excess, moderation in everything, were principles of the educated mind. The people who coined the term *harmonia* applied it in their personal life—the life of body and soul—thus *nous ygies en somati ygies*, a healthy mind in a healthy body; in the relations between order and freedom, religious unity and rational individualism, nationalism and universalism, individual rights and community obligations.[11]

Whether *harmonia* remained a yearning of an ideal or became a realized experience, it was born as a result of conflicts and dialogues between thought and experience, faith and reason, mythical symbolism and historical realities. For example, the conflict between monarchy and oligarchy, oligarchy and the *demos* gave birth to democracy. And democracy is a system which harmonizes extremes and brings equality among people of diverse interests and different talents. The debate between the ideas expressed by Pericles in his famous *Funeral Oration* and those of Plato's *Republic* affects our life today. Democracy or Monarchy? Democracy or Dictatorship? Democracy or Oligarchy? are questions of perennial significance.

Several more important and relevant ideas were emphasized in pre-classical Greece. Self-control, fidelity and trust in married life, hospitality toward all no matter what the origin, color, or creed of the person in need of hospitality, generosity, righteousness, respect for the elders, but also *eros* as the beginning of trust between husband and wife. No wonder the Homeric epics were considered a gospel among the ancient Greeks and are studied to the present day as classics, not only as epic poetry but also as sources for the study of the social and moral values of the ancient Greeks.

The human being was perceived as both a spiritual, divinely ordained person, but also as an intellectual earthly being. The later was the result of the presence of reason (*logos*), but reason was not the ultimate in human conduct. There is something deeper and autonomous in the human *psyche*, a *daimonion*, a spirit of supernatural origins. Their investigation and study of the nature of the human led them to the conclusion of God's or the Divinity's existence. Thus the affinity between the universal *Logos* and human *logos*, the affinity between the Divine and the human. At no times were the ancient Greeks anthropocentric but throughout their long history they combined theocentricism and anthropocentricism, a synergy, if you please, between Divinity and humanity. At no time was Greek civilization only man-centered for it was deity-centered also. Some of their artistic and literary productions were celebrations of both Divinity and humanity. And their earliest, the Ionian, or Pre-Socratic, philosophers believed that their knowledge and wisdom derived from or were gifts of the Divinity. The human being as a spiritual and intellectual being has metaphysical roots. "Men are gods, and gods are men . . . god in man and man in god" said Herakleitos.[12] "A mystery indeed" said approvingly the Christian theologian (second century) Clement of Alexandria.[13]

The interrelationship between the divine and the human was later expressed by Pindar, the greatest of the Greek Lyric poets who believed that whatever is excellent in the human being is partly inborn, a gift of the gods. He believed that in the realm of the spirit, the divine and the human met.[14]

The idea of the nature of the human achieved a climax in the thought of Socrates, Plato, and Plotinos. All three emphasized the divine destiny of the human being as a soul or spiritual entity. The question was raised What is man, and What powers and properties distinguish such a nature from any other.[15] As a god-related being, man should not submit to the desires of mortal nature but should seek to take flight from the world of evil to the other, that means "becoming like the divine so far as man can, becoming righteous with the help of wisdom." "Nothing is more like the divine than any one of us who becomes as righteous as possible. It is here that a man shows his true spirit and power or lack of spirit and nothingness" adds Socrates.[16] The human as a spiritual being related to the Divinity longs to return to it.

Christianity's notion about the presence of the divine in the human and the ultimate destiny of the human to be eternally in God was not foreign to the ancient Greeks. In the Second Letter of Peter, Christians are called upon to become sharers in the divine nature through faith, courage, self control, and virtue with knowledge (2 Pet 1.5). "If one knows himself, he will know God; and knowing God, he will be made like God" wrote later Clement of Alexandria.[17] Indeed there are many common teachings between Greek philosophy and the Christian scriptures. Thus Deacon Agapetos ventured to say:

> He who knows himself will know God; and he who knows God will be made like to God; and he will be made like to God who has become worthy of God; and he becomes worthy of God, who does nothing unworthy of God, but he thinks the things that are his, and speaks what he thinks, and does what he speaks.[18]

III

The third major idea of the ancient Greeks of concern to us was about the human mind (the *nous*), reason, which was expected to be not only for basic needs of the individual and his community, but also for problems pertaining to major issues such as international relations, rights of minorities, individual values in conflict with the state, and more.

The idea of thinking rightly, logically, was of paramount significance to the ancient Greeks, and it remains to the present day a principle of great value for all human beings. But what does it mean to think rightly? It means "not to think wrongly!" "Not to think wrongly is the greatest gift of god" to man writes Aeschylos in his *Agamemnon*.[19] While Aeschylos sees right thinking as a gift of god, Socrates, Plato and others after them, emphasized that to think rightly is to see everything in its proper perspective and examine it in its natural place. In the last analysis the Greeks emphasized that human beings should know their limitations, their abilities and place in the universe, to remember that they are mortals and behave accordingly. "Know thyself" was one of their famous maxims.

In Plato's *Phaedo*, Socrates turned to his favorite disciple Crito and gave this advice: ". . . dear Crito, . . . not to think rightly about a thing not only puts one into a false relationship with the thing itself, but it also works some evil in one's soul."[20] So man must think rightly about the divinity, about himself/ herself, and about everything else as it was meant by nature to be. Man must obey the laws of nature and accept himself as he really is. For the Greeks to assure prerogatives belonging to god, or nature, was an unforgivable arrogance, a hubris, leading to ruin and destruction. Thinking rightly implies feeling rightly about the self, nature, other fellow human beings. A person's "conduct and attitude toward anything inevitably gravitate to the level of his thinking and feeling about it." Do we need to explore further how this great idea affects us today? Consider how Hitler's Germany, Stalin's and other totalitarian states regarded other people and the consequences of their thinking. Indeed the necessity to think and feel rightly about fellow human beings, nature, and environment is accentuated by the present temper and attitude of humankind in general and of the Americans in particular. Using the mind, thinking and feeling rightly about the family of human beings, the order and laws of nature are necessary presuppositions for right attitude, action, and conduct toward them.

IV

The fourth idea discusses the concept of dialogue. It is one of the major inventions of the ancient Greeks which affects us today in a very positive way. Dialogue, from the Greek *dialogos*, means talking together, an interchange and discussion of ideas openly and frankly seeking mutual understanding, harmony, peace. The steering wheel in any dialogue is the *logos*, reason. Whether in the classroom between students and teachers, in the United Nations between representatives of states, or the World Council of Churches between theologians of Christian communions, the dialogue is one of the major strengths of the twentieth century family of nations.

The dialogue is the basis of the dialectic method and it was elevated to the state of the art of persuasion by Socrates. In Plato's Crito, Socrates and Crito are engaged in a conversation concerning the legitimacy of Socrates' escape from the prison.[21] Crito encouraged Socrates to escape because the court had unjustly condemned his teacher to death. Socrates argued that it was his duty to abide by the law and that it is wrong to retaliate evil for evil. Retaliation for any injustice is always wrong he argues. Incompatible assumptions, differences of opinions can be resolved through intelligent and civilized manners and dialogues. The personal sense of right and wrong, self-righteousness, and self-illusions can be dissipated when we are engaged in a dialogic exploration of the issues.

In recent years, whether in international relations or inter religious and interfaith conferences, the scope and meaning of dialogue has been expanded for the better. Global education for cooperation and peace cannot ignore our knowledge of, and relation with, people of other countries, races, religious creeds, political and economic systems. The desire to prevent a holocaust of cosmic dimensions and secure the cooperation of members of the human family has brought the leaders of the superpowers to dialogues. Monologues are dangerous while dialogues generate reconsideration and rethinking on issues and problems which divide nations, communities, and families. Issues of human rights and global interdependence, and ethnic and social conflicts can be resolved when we pursue deliberate, extensive, and sustained dialogues. In Plato's dialogues Socrates reminds us to question our assumptions and be in constant dialogue with ourselves and fellow human beings.

V

The fifth idea about the right of free speech was introduced very early in Greek history. Homer relates that in an assembly of the Greeks in Troy an ordinary commander named Thersites, "with a mind of subversive ideas and opposition to those in authority" kept criticizing "at the top of his lungs," Agamemnon, his commander-in-chief. Thersites was reprimanded by Odysseus, but he was not prevented from voicing his opinions.[22]

In the eighth century, Hesiod became the outspoken champion for the oppressed farmers. He challenged the wealthy to be more considerate of the poor and reprimanded the slothful poor, creating an atmosphere for a free exchange of ideas and a dialogue. Hesiod was pessimistic of human nature, especially when possessed with arrogance, injustice, crafty lying, of kindness, self-respect, and consideration for others. He preached a code of hard work, self-reliance, honesty, thrift, good friends, moderation, and religious observance.[23] Soon after Hesiod, individual moral values were emphasized by other authors. The fables ascribed to Aesop (ca. 650?) underlined the ideas of honesty, moderation, tolerance, and humility in the sense of self-knowledge.

VI

Closely related to their idea of free speech were their ideas about *isonomia* and *democratia*, the sixth of the main ideas under analysis. Both have affected and continue to concern every free state of the Western World. *Isonomia*, an idea introduced by Solon, the sixth century chief archon of Athens, means equality under law, equality of political rights for all citizens and *democratia*, introduced in sixth century Athens, means the power is in the hands of the *demos*—the people.

Isonomia, equality under law, was one of the major legal ideas introduced by Solon. As chief archon of Athens he arbitrated a crucial conflict between the rich landowners and the poor farmers. He put into practice the principle of *isonomia* "so that neither side should have an unfair advantage over the other." He stated and practiced for the first time the theory that government should be impartial in the treatment of its citizens, reconciling conflicting interests. "Equality under law breeds no revolution" he said.[24] Equality and moderation were never better practiced than by the legislator Solon, who introduced several more democratic elements in sixth century Greece.

Solon's sense of happiness is associated with his understanding of moderation, equality, honor, and a sense of responsibility. When he was asked by Kroesos, the wealthy king of Lydia whom he considered the happiest man he had known, expecting to hear praises about his wealth, Solon replied:

> "I consider the happiest person Tellos of Athens. To begin with, his city was prosperous. He had a family of attractive and responsible sons, who in turn had children, all of whom survived. He had enough means to live comfortably, according to our modest standards. Finally, he met death nobly, for in a battle . . . he came to the rescue of his countrymen and helped rout the enemy before he fell; and the Athenians gave him a state funeral with a hero's honors."[25]

Solon's wisdom and theory about the value of arbitration in social conflicts, and his condemnation of poverty as the source of social uprisings, was followed to advantage in later Greek domestic conflicts and interstate disputes. His ideas exerted a major influence upon later Greek philosophers. Two and a half centuries later Aristotle called poverty "the greatest defect of democracy" and the one single cause of social conflicts and revolts.[26] Do we need to comment on whether Solon and Aristotle were right? Indeed, poverty continues to be the greatest defect of our democracy, with more than 38,000,000 Americans living in poverty, and 3,000,000 in the streets and subways of our cities.

Freedom of speech and equality are major elements of *democratia*. *Democratia*, from which we have the term democracy, means that power resides with the majority of the citizens, neither with one ruler (monarchy), nor with a few aristocrats (aristocracy, oligarchy). Democracy was born and practiced in Athens and in many other city-states of ancient Greece. The merits, advantages, and responsibilities of the citizens in a democracy are movingly described by Pericles, the chief archon of fifth century Athens, in his famous funeral oration.

In a democracy all people deserve to have equal rights before the law; individuals, regardless of their political, economic, or social position should be recognized only on the basis of their merit. Democracy respects an individual's privacy and recognizes not only the value of written laws but also of unwritten or natural laws. In a democracy all issues receive full and open discussion before decisions are reached. In a democracy there are no restrictions even upon foreigners who visit the state. Athens became the school of Hellas because it believed in a liberal education for all its citizens; because it offered religious, dramatic, musical, and athletic festivals "to cheer the heart and refresh the spirit" of all, in the words of Pericles.

But in a democracy, citizens have responsibilities. Wealth, for example, was regarded as a means for public service rather than for ostentatious private display, and citizens were expected to take their political duties seriously. Those who refused to participate in public and state affairs were regarded as *idiotes*, from which our idiot derives. Pericles stressed that "happiness depends on freedom, and freedom is won and preserved by courage." The whole of Pericles' oration needs to be studied carefully by every college student and citizen.

Even with this short resume it is sufficient to recognize that many of the principles of Athenian democracy have affected our own democracy. Several of the Fathers of the early American republic were students of classical Greece. It has been said that Abraham Lincoln used Pericles' oration to inspire him for his Gettysburg Address. Whatever the historical truth, Athenian democracy remains an inspiration and a model for a direct democracy.

VII

Literature constitutes a mirror of a people's mind, thought, ideas, social and national issues, and problems for it often emerges out of a direct experience of the writer. English literature owes very much to Greek literary forms, and Greek mythology is ever present in it. Greek literature whether epic poetry, history, philosophy, or drama was didactic in nature. Two central ideas dominate Greek literature: one reveals the perpetual search of the Greeks for meaning, and the second's objective was to teach man how to live well.

The great victories of the Greeks against the numerically superior Persians in the fifth century gave the Greeks self-confidence, the security of freedom, and the opportunity to think and reflect. The fifth century gave birth to brilliant minds such as Aeschylos, Sophocles, Euripides, Pheidias, Pericles, Themistocles, Protagoras, Xenophanes, Socrates, Plato, and many more. It was in the fifth century that the idea of the intelligent person matured, the person of a free creative mind, a person insatiably curious and powerfully creative.[27]

In the course of the fifth and fourth centuries B.C. the Greek mind searched for new expressions of its power in political thought, philosophy, art and architecture, medicine, and other areas of human endeavor. Human reason, seen as unlimited, probed the universe, questioned the existence of mythological gods, provided new understanding of the divinity, searched for meaning in the mystery of the cosmos and the mystery of human existence. These new ideas created a tension with the old established traditions. The plays of Sophocles, in particular *Oedipus the King*, *Oedipus at Colonus*, and *Antigone*, are the best mirrors of the classical age. The heroes of these plays are images of the critical spirit in search of meaning. In the words of an outstanding authority on Sophocles, the hero of Sophocles "investigates, examines, questions, infers . . . knows, finds, reveals, makes clear, demonstrates, learns, teaches, liberates, and saves."[28] Political and social problems, religious questions and issues concerning character, fate, and destiny, the authority of tradition and their relationship between private conscience and state laws, individual rights and community norms—all became subject of questioning and search for meaning.

It is very difficult for any student of fifth century B.C. Athens, and indeed of the Greek world from the opening of the sixth century to the closing of the fourth, not to call it a market of ideas. While many of the ideas from the 600s to the middle of the fifth century, were speculative and abstract, Socrates introduced ideas of a pragmatic nature. The question he raised again and again was "how should man live," what is the nature of a good and happy live. To live well meant to think rightly about God—god as natural law, conscience, mind, reason—the cosmos, including the immediate environment, and fellow human beings. The ideas of Socrates, Plato, Aristotle, and Zeno possessed a close union between physical and metaphysical life, morals and religion. Platonic metaphysics in particular, Aristotelian logic, and Stoic ethics have exerted a tremendous influence on the Christian and non-Christian religious philosophy of Western Civilization. Faith that truth is our best friend, and that the knowledge of truth is not beyond man's reach are principles that affect the life of many of us today. Faith in honest searching, faith in honest inquiry is in the heart of our education. *"Olbios ostis tes historias eschen mathesin,"* "happy is the person who has learnt the value of inquiry" writes Euripides.[29]

The idea that there should be co-operation between reason and belief, and knowledge and faith is one which preoccupied the Greek mind for many centuries. Sophocles' play, *Oedipus the King,* is a brilliant illustration of the conflict between reason and belief, innovation, and tradition. Oedipus viewed reason alone as the ultimate principle that should rule, and man as the measure of all things. Teiresias, the prophet, reminded Oedipus that religious belief, natural law, and traditional faith should be taken seriously because they are divine realities.

Much has been said about Greek rationalism, and that in Greek thought man is the measure of all things, a maxim extensively used in recent years by secular humanists. The maxim has been attributed to the philosopher Protagoras who wrote: "Man is the measure of all things, of the things that are, how they are, and the things that are not, how they are not." But it has been rightly observed that Protagoras' philosophy was not totally anthropocentric. Faith in a supernatural power, and a divinity, or divinities, was never absent from any period of Greek history and thought. Their faith in human intelligence, reason, and rigorous and rational action did not indicate lack of belief in something beyond themselves. In Homer's *Odyssey* and Aeschylos' *Prometheus Bound* we have a celebration of man's triumph over his environment; in Sophocles' *Antigone* we see a high praise for man's restless and unmitigated will and determination; but in Euripides' *Suppliants* we have an indication of how miserable man can be by relying and misusing the gifts he has received. The lesson from Sophocles' *Oedipus the King* is that after all God is the measure of all things. Isocrates and some sophists considered man as the measure of all things but at no time were all the Greeks in agreement. Plato was closer to the truth when he emphasized that the Greek spirit from Homer to his own times saw "God rather than man should be the measure of all things for man."[30] Religious rather than secular humanism prevailed in the thought of the ancient Greeks.

VIII

Conscience as a balanced force, regulating the relationships between Divinity and humanity was the great idea promoted by Stoic philosophy. Conscience is god's unwritten law in the human being. But man is also endowed with reason. The two must work in harmony. Several ethical principles of Stoicism exerted a tremendous influence on the mind of late antiquity, including early Christian theology. Conscience played a crucial part in Saint Paul's argument in Romans 2.12-15. Paul enumerates elsewhere virtues as the fruit of the spirit, which in actuality are virtues stressed in the Stoic tradition (Gal. 5.22-23). The Stoic views of accountability and judgment seem to have influenced Paul's eschatology as well.[31]

Because of their emphasis on the excellent efficacy of reason and conscience, the Greeks reconciled the claims of the individual in the state, the idea of the personal versus the public good; the freedom of the individual but also the devotion of the citizen to the state, of the government and the interests of the governed, the rights of the individual, and the rights of the community.

The basic intuition of love for a fellow human being (*philanthropia*) energized and revitalized by the ethic of *agape* was adopted by Christianity and was transmitted to the civilization of western Europe and indeed America. *Philanthropia*, a synonym for *agape,* is perhaps the most successful of man's evolutionary experiments. A humanity without philanthropy is *therianthropic*—(beastly) humanity. The ethical imperatives of self-control and moderation, and the consciousness of the human frailty and mortality led to the development of the noble idea of *philanthropia.* The Greeks had three terms to describe what we call love, or charity. *Philanthropia* derives from *philein ton anthropon*—to love the human being, for the reason that the object of love is a fellow human being.[32] *Eros* means to desire, to yearn for. It was used to describe the force which brings together the male and the female elements of the human being and procreate their kind. Later it assumed a mystical meaning to denote the desire of the human to unite with the ultimate being. And the third term for love is *agape.* It expressed a concept of love identified with a warm, altruistic selfless love. It is this term of *agape* used by Saint Paul in his famous thirteenth chapter of his first letter to the Corinthians:

> If I speak in the tongues of men and of angels, but do not have love, I am a noisy gong or a clanging cymbal. And if I have prophetic powers, and understand all mysteries and all knowledge, and if I have all faith, so as to remove mountains, but do not have love, I am nothing. If I give away all my possessions, and if I deliver my body to be burned, but do not have love, I gain nothing. Love is patient; love is kind; love is not envious or boastful; it is not arrogant or rude. Love does not insist on its own way; it is not irritable or resentful; it does not rejoice in wrongdoing, but rejoices in the truth. Love bears all things, believes all things, hopes all things, endures all things. (1 Cor. 13.1-7)

Whether in the sense of *philanthropia, eros,* or *agape,* the Greeks believed that love is *theocentric*—it derives from God, it manifests the divinity's love for the creation including man, and that it should be imitated by human beings in their own relationships. The time came when *philanthropia* and *agape* were used interchangeably. Both began as theocentric concepts and evolved into anthropocentric concerns, what we call today philanthropy and love.

In his *Prometheus Bound*, Aeschylos writes that god Prometheus brought fire to humankind in order to teach them arts and handicrafts, to help them survive. And he did this out of love for humankind. "Behold me a doomed god, enchained . . . because of my very great *philanthropia* for men."[33] Several years later after Aeschylos, Plato, too, defined *philanthropia* as the love of God for humanity. The divinity intervened through *daemonia*, spirits, in order to establish peace and justice among men and free them from feuds and wars, Plato writes.[34] Other Greek thinkers such as Xenophon emphasized that it is out of *philanthropia* for humankind that men enjoy goods and provisions, weather and the seasons of the year, the moon and the stars, water and fire, and the whole beautiful cosmos.[35]

And what was the origins and function of agape? In the Platonic Socrates' discussion of the nature and function of love, Diotima, the priestess from Mantinea provides the answer: Love, being both human and divine

> is an intermediate Spirit whose function
> is to mediate between gods and men,
> conveying to the gods men's prayers and sacrifices,
> and interpreting to men the injunctions of the gods
> and their rewards to men for the sacrifices they offer

Agape came to mean several things such as love for beauty, wisdom, goodness, and desire for procreation and spiritual attainment. Philanthropy as an act of giving to the needy and institutions promoting the welfare of the community; *eros* as the supreme drive that unites the two halves of the human being in order to reconstruct a new one; and *agape* as the ultimate force which mediates, reconciles, and promotes better relations between individuals and societies are supreme ideas that continue to affect us today. Philanthropy should not be practiced as a mere social obligation, or for the cause of vanity and selfish gains, but as a real concern for the welfare of fellow human beings. *Eros* is a healthy and creative power which unfortunately has been misunderstood and terribly abused, commercialized, and degenerated into sexual hedonism rather than a recreative and sublime power both physical and spiritual. "*Agape* as an intermediate Spirit whose function is to convey men's prayers and sacrifices to the gods, and to interpret in turn the injunctions and replies of the gods to men,"[36] in the words of Diotima, reminds us of the concept of love in the Christian Bible. It is because of love for the salvation of the human that God becomes man in order to raise man to divinity (Jn. 3.16). Whether in its Greek rational or Christian spiritual intuitive, *agape*—love remains "the most potent factor in achieving the best human relationship."

IX

While many of the ideas of the ancient Greeks were theoretical, practical and experimental ideas on the physical nature of the universe were not absent from them. From the fifth century through the fourth century B.C. into the Hellenistic, theories included those of the physical sciences such as those which spoke of the elements, atoms, kinetic energy, scientific medicine, astronomy, anatomy, geography, and geometry.

The nature of this essay does not allow us to illustrate every one of these scientific areas whether theoretical or experiential. Here are a few scientific ideas. Parmenides' ideas about Being and Not Being are quite timely. He writes: "Being is real, Non—Being is impossible...." Being is without beginning or end; it includes everything, is immovable and eternal, one continuous whole. How could it have been created? From what could it have come into existence, and how? It cannot have come from nothing.[37] The atomic theory was not introduced in the 1940s. Some 2500 years ago Leukippos wrote that "atoms (individual particles) and their countless combinations are the elements of everything; they are unlimited in number, and are in continuous motion. The solid and compact atoms may be defined as "Being," and they move through empty space, which may be called "Not Being." His views were further developed by

Democritos[38] and it took mankind 2,500 years to prove them wrong that the atom cannot be split.

The Hippocratic oath includes ethical principles which affect modern medicine and guide many physicians in their daily practice. It reads as follows:

> I swear . . . that according to my ability I will keep this oath: to regard the man who taught me the art of medicine as dear to me as my own parents; to follow that system of treatment which I believe will help my patients, and to refrain from anything that is harmful to them. I will give no deadly drug if I am asked to do so, nor will I recommend any such thing; I will not practice abortion. In purity and holiness I will practice the art of medicine. Whatever I see or hear which should not be divulged, I will keep secret. While I continue to keep this oath may I enjoy life and the practice of my profession, respected at all times by all men.[39]

Hippocrates' medical ethics influenced for many centuries Christian and non-Christian physicians alike. Thus a pagan physician of late antiquity, identified as Pseudo-Hipparchos, advised fellow-physicians as follows:

> I charge you not to show yourselves inhuman, but to take the wealth or poverty [of the patient] into account, in certain cases even to treat them *gratis* and to consider future gratitude more than present fame. If, therefore, the summons for aid happens to be the case of an unknown or impecunious man, he is most of all to be assisted; for wherever there is love to one's neighbor, it means readiness to act.[40]

Euclid's geometric principles and demonstrations are studied to the present day in our schools. Some of his axioms have survived as maxims. "Equals of the same thing are equal to each other." "If equals be added to equals, the wholes are equal." "Parallels to the same straight line are also parallel to each other."

Archimedes was the greatest of experimental scientists of ancient times. He was able to separate the science of geometry

from the art of mechanics. It is acknowledged that he antici-
pated the calculus and that he employed the principles of higher
algebra. His mechanics have classified him among the scientific geniuses of history. Some of the men whose contributions
affect us today can only be mentioned: Aristarchos of Samos
was the first to speak of the heliocentric system. Erasistratos
of Chios became the father of physiology making important
observations about the circulatory system and the nervous system. Eratosthenes of Cyrene was the first who calculated with
a high degree of accuracy the circumference of the earth."His
method was sound, and his result was astonishingly accurate."
In his calculations he fell short by some 20 miles. Hipparchos
of Nicaea was the greatest astronomer and the first to define
the time of the year. Hierophilos of Samos was the father of
anatomy and Heracleides of Pontos, the father of pharmacol-
ogy.[41]

Some of the ideas of the Hellenistic age, whether through
Stoicism, Epicurianism or other schools of thought, have survived as maxims and continue to influence people. The idea
that "a man must stand erect, not be kept erect by others" is an
inheritance from Stoicism. The Greeks loved to harmonize opposite forces bringing a balance between them.

X

The idea of evil is as old as the human being. Homer relates
that Achilles tells Priam that Zeus has two casks, one filled
with good things, and the other with bad, and that he gives to
men out of each according to his pleasure.[42] But Zeus rejected
this and complained that men do attribute their sufferings and
the existence of evil itself to the gods, but they do it falsely,
because human beings are the cause of their own sorrows.

Later Greek thought stressed that whatever we call evil, or
the nature of evil, does not exist. Evil is not a part of the consti-
tution or nature of things, for if there were a principal source of
evil it would be good, for the first cause, or the primary source,
is good. Ancient Greek thought rejected a dualism—a god of
good and a god of evil. "As a mark is not set up for the purpose
of missing it, so neither does the nature of evil exist in the

Universe," writes Epictetos. Evil is to live contrary to nature, to violate what is natural to man's own nature and the nature of the universe. What is contrary to reason is also an act contrary to nature; what is contrary to the dictates of human conscience is contrary to the indwelling divinity.

Closely related to the idea of evil is the idea of the good life, good life means to live in conformity with the self and nature. "How shall man live?" was a question raised again and again by Socrates. The good life is a life of virtue and virtue is a product of knowledge of good and evil; a life of justice, or the giving to every person his/her due; a life of fortitude, temperance, and moderation in all things. Aristotle equated the good life with the fullest development of man's spiritual and intellectual capability for the good and virtue, and virtue has its rewards: For virtue only of all human things takes her reward not from the hands of others. "Virtue herself rewards virtue," writes an anonymous ancient Greek poet.[43]

Plato writes that the virtuous person achieves a perfect life, attains the proper perspective of the universe, and the vision of the idea of the Absolute Good (God). Indeed "business ethics," "medical ethics," and trends in other areas of ethical concern should echo of Plato's call for the ideal society and the ideal person in an ideal state. Plato's, Aristotle's, Zeno's, and Epictetus' teachings about the good human life and its relations to a harmonious universe, or the environment, are ever timely. Ancient Greek thought includes a philosophy which can be common human experience. It remains a reservoir of ideas and principles which can be used by human beings, if only they decided to participate in it.[44]

To avoid evil and live well in harmony with the self, nature, and divinity—divinity as conscience, mind, and reason—man must seek the truth, and the knowledge of truth is not beyond man's reach even though the Greeks acknowledged that human inquiry has its limits.

XI

One of the great ideas of the ancient Greeks is about *paideia*. In an age of computers and high technology, one may wonder how Greek *paideia* affects our life today. *Paideia* means education, and education has been defined as "the process by which a community preserves and transmits its physical and intellectual character."[45] The basis of education is the consciousness of values we possess as guideposts of our lives—religious, moral, artistic, and political. However lightly we value the achievements of other civilizations, the educational ideals and the deliberate pursuit of Western civilization's ideals begin with Greece.

But *paideia* is more than principles of education, learning—it is mental culture, character formation, and character formation meant the creation of a real and genuine human being. The ideal of the educated person was the political person, not the *idiotis*, the idiot; the person who shaped the community and was shaped by the community. The fundamental educational ideals of the ancient Greeks included thinking rightly, reasonable assumptions, a dialogic approach to issues and problems that divide persons, communities, and nations; a constant inquiry as a foundation for knowledge.

Greek *paideia* as the sum total of principles that contribute to the formation of the really educated person cannot be treated in a paragraph or two, but I need to emphasize that I share the views expressed by Allan Bloom, Saul Bellow, and others who have appealed for a reconsideration of recent trends in our educational philosophy and practice. The ancient Greeks "believed that education embodies the purpose of all human effort . . . and . . . the ultimate justification for the existence of both the individual and the community," in the words of the best authority on Greek paideia.[46] Is there anyone who doubts that more than high technology we need highly civilized human beings?

Socrates taught that it is more ethical to be treated unjustly than to treat anyone unjustly; to constantly question our assumptions and to think and act rightly. In the last analysis the Delphic maxim "know thyself" meant that every human being must think rightly about the self, the community, the laws of life, nature and divinity; to have a clear understanding of the strengths and weakness, the abilities and limitations of humanity; educated is the person who is truly human. "*Os harien est' anthropos an anthropos*"—accomplished and elegant is the person who possesses true humanity—writes the fourth century poet Menander.[47] An educated person is expected to honor the human being as such; to be educated and to be human became synonymous. Education remains our only true possession. When Demetrios Poliorketes asked Stilpon (ca. 380-300 B.C.) the philosopher to list all the things he lost during the plundering of his house in Megara, Stilpon answered: "Nobody was able to carry off my education."[48]

XII

The last of the major ideas of ancient Greece, with which I wish to conclude this essay, is the idea about the *logos*. The term *logos* has been given a variety of meanings, such as word, speech, rational faculty, proposition, principle, and reason. *Logos* as principle and reason has exerted a tremendous influence on western civilization and it continues to affect the life of millions of people who accept the historic person of Jesus of Nazareth as the preexistent *Logos*, the Christ of history and the founder of the Christian movement.

The gospel according to John opens with a most important affirmation of the Greek concept of the logos which was first introduced by the sixth century B.C. Greek philosopher Heraclitos. For Heraclitos, *Logos* denotes the first principle which brought the universe into being. The reality of the *Logos* is analogous to the *logos* (reason) in the human being which regulates and serves as the source of all human law and life. The conception was used later by Plato and Aristotle, but it was more fully developed by Zeno and the Stoic philosophers. In late antiquity *Logos* came to mean the active force in the universe, a purposive cosmic reason, a Divine Reason, God's *nous*, or mind, which is both transcendent and immanent, creative and providential. It is transcendent because it is exterior, beyond comprehension; and it is immanent because it is interior, a personal agency and the elder son of God who played an active and creative role in the cosmos.

In the Christian theological tradition this understanding of the Greek *Logos* was identified with the preexistence, creative, illuminating, and redemptive work of Christ the *Logos*. "In the beginning was the *Logos* and the Logos was with God, and the *Logos* was God. He was in the beginning with God; all things were made through him, and without him was not anything made that was made" (Jn. 1: 1-3). Thus *Logos* is God in action, creating, revealing, redeeming.

The author of the gospel used Greek philosophical categories to make the belief about the person of Jesus the Messiah of Matthew's gospel understood by those familiar with Greek thought, who knew of the preexistent *logos*. Though there are differing opinions, I subscribe to the exegesis which sees in the Prologue of John's Gospel "a phrasing of the Christian message in Hellenistic terms to catch the interest of Greek readers."[49] The evangelist assumed that his readers knew the conception of *Logos* as the Divine *Logos*, the universal mind by which the cosmos came into being and is sustained by it. In Hellenized Judaism, in Philo for example, *Logos* meant the rational principle but also Divine Wisdom as in Proverbs 8.22-31. Thus Christ was also called "the 'Wisdom of God' " (1 Cor. 1.24; 30).

Whatever the interpretation of the term logos may be, it is certain that Christianity became a universal religion because it borrowed and used Greek ideas and concepts in order to make its message acceptable by the non-Hebrew nations. For more than four hundred years, the Mediterranean world had come under the influence of Greek thought and Greek was the universal or spoken language. Thought and language are inseparable. It is through Christianity then that the profound concept of *logos* (or *Logos*) has influenced Western civilization and affects us even today.

Epilogue

In summary, Greek ideas in religion, philosophy, art, and politics have profoundly modified the whole trend of modern civilization. Ancient Greece (archaic, classical, Hellenistic, Roman, and Byzantine) has imposed her thought, standards, literary forms, imagery, visions, and dreams wherever she is known. The extent of the Greek influence is incalculable throughout Europe and its intensity is at its highest in Germany, England, and France. Numerous books have been written about "Greek cultural imperialism" over Germany and Victorian England.

The Greek ethical standard is associated with Greek art and architecture and has emphasized the greatness of spirit, nobility, simplicity, serenity of soul, and religious and racial tolerance.

Just a few remarks on the impact of Greek architecture and art on the American republic of the early 19th century.

In its efforts to repudiate British influences, the Fathers of the young Republic rejected the Georgian tradition of architecture and searched for an architectural style more appropriate to a free people. This led to the Greek Revival. The chief forerunner, indeed, the architect, of the Greek Revival was Thomas Jefferson, who preferred the Romanized style of Greek architecture. Jefferson and other exponents of the Greek revival believed that there was an intimate connection between the building methods of the ancient Greeks and their democratic ideals. By 1820 the Greek Revival spread throughout the whole country. It became almost obligatory that Federal and State government building, banks, libraries, universities, and the better private homes should have columns like those of the Parthenon or other Greek temples.

The art that adorns the Capitol in Washington is no less indicative of the influences of ancient Greek art. The sparkling and colorful frescoes of the Capitol reflect the ideals of the early Americans and symbolize the themes of "life, liberty, and the pursuit of happiness." The thirteen maidens, which represent the original states, and many designs and scenes painted on the Senate side of the Capitol are taken from Greek mythology. The painter, Constantino Brumidi, was immersed in the classical tradition. In a copy of the Bible given to him by the American Bible Society upon his arrival in New York he wrote "Constantino Brumidi, son of Stavro of the province of Arcadia in the Peloponnesos of Greece, and of Anna Bianchini of Rome."[50]

The Greek religious mind has seen the divine spirit of the *Logos* unfolding like a flower in all the races on earth. From as early as the Homeric age to the closing of the school of philosophy in Athens by Emperor Justinian in 529, the Greek mind recognized many divine powers in one divine cosmos. Their poets, philosophers, historians possessed the sense of the universal divine presence and the holiness of the universe. What Sophocles said about his native village can be expanded to include the thought of later centuries and of the whole universe: "all the place is holy, and there is nothing which is without a share of soul."[51]

This perception of holiness prepared the ground for the development of monotheism under the great Neoplatonist philosophers of the early Christian era which, however, included polytheistic elements. For example, Plotinos sees a multiplicity of gods emanating from the One, the *Nous* or Divine Intellect; the One "encompasses in himself all things immortal, every intellect, every god, every *soul*."[52] The last phase of ancient Greek thought was expressed by Simplikios, the last major of the non-Christian philosophers. In his commentary on the *Enchiridion* of Epictetos, Simplikios writes:

> The Good is source and principle of all beings. For that which all things desire, and to which all things reach up, this is the principle and the goal of all things. And the Good brings forth all things from himself."[53]

So the searching person who aspires to know and unite with this unknown Good, or God, should strive to have a more immediate relationship with more accessible beings created by the Unknown God.

Throughout their spiritual life and religious evolution, the Greeks have searched to find the divine presence. And they searched for it in their mountains and valleys, their seas and rivers, their villages and cities, their trees and springs. And they found the divine presence in the likeness of many distinct beings and yet united with the one, the Unknowable. This element is very much alive in Greek Orthodox piety today, as well as in Orthodox theology which sees God's activity in the Incarnate *Logos*.[54] Don't you think that our seas and rivers, our mountains and lakes, our cities and towns, our environment in general would appreciate such an understanding by their modern masters—human beings and technology alike?

On the other hand, political continues to mean the belief that a citizen has rights and duties in the *polis*, the state. Monarchy, oligarchy and aristocracy, and democracy are governmental systems applied in ancient Greece and being practiced to the present day. But what kind of democracy do we have when our governments are elected by less than 40% of the electorate? Is our system a democracy or an aristocracy? Just two questions for reflection.

There are so many philosophical ideas in ancient Greece which prompted the great mathematician and philosopher Alfred North Whitehead to say that western philosophy is nothing but footnotes to Plato's thought. And the leading American philosopher Allan Bloom writes: "What is essential about . . . any of the Platonic dialogues, is reproducible in almost all times and places."[55] Numerous literary forms in English and American literature continue to depend either on Greek mythology, poetry, drama, tragedy, satire, or the Bible.

As Isokrates, the fourth century B.C. moralist and educator, had observed, Greece had ceased to be a geographical area. Not only the numerous Greek city-states, spread all over the Mediterranean world, but also the intellectual activities of the Greeks had made their country a land without boundaries and a civilization without limits.

On the one hand, through Alexander the Great's expeditions, Greek civilization extended deeply and widely into the Near and Middle East—the interior of eastern Asia Minor, Syria, Palestine, Egypt, Mesopotamia, Persia, and as far as the seventh century of our era when it was absorbed by Islam. On the other hand, Rome took up the mission of extending Hellenism over the Western part of the Mediterranean. East and West were permeated with Greek art, architecture, literature, philosophy, religion. Hellenized Rome and Hellenized Judaism, through Christianity, preserved and disseminated many ideas of the ancient Greeks. "Shakespeare we trace through the Latins to Menander; Milton through Vergil to Homer and Theokritos, Bacon to Aristotle, Sir Thomas More to Plato," in the words of a modern authority.[56]

No less than through modern Greece, its people and language, its social and political values, its poetry, its popular culture and folklore, Greek history is not closed. "The more we study modern Greece, the more we are convinced that the Hellenic race is by no means extinct." Every phase of Greek history has to show its achievements and its failures. "The Modern Greeks have not only produced great poets; in their war of independence and in their recent resistance movements to foreign invaders, they have performed feats of heroism that are as fine as their ancestors' feats at Marathon and at Thermopylae, while, on a more mundane plane, they have played a highly successful part in the Modern World's commercial life," in the words of Arnold Toynbee, perhaps the most authoritative scholar of the history of the Greeks from remote antiquity to the present.[57]

To be sure the persistence of ancient Greek ideas and values, including the language itself, is of importance not only for the modern Greeks but also for all the inheritors of the classical tradition. It indicates fidelity to the past but also the legitimacy, its seriousness, and the unity of Western Civilization's historical experience.

Notes

[1] Pindaros, *Pythian Odes*, 5.25.

[2] Cf. Gilbert Murray, *Five Stages of Greek Religion* (New York: Doubleday, 1955), pp. 66-72; Jean-Pierre Vernant, "Greek Religion" in *Religions of Antiquity*, ed. by Robert M. Seltzer (New York: Macmillan Co., 1989) 164-65.

[3] Heracleitos, *Fragments*, no. 78.

[4] Menander, *Fragments*, no. 549k; 535, 536.

[5] Homer, *The Odyssey*, Bks 3 and 4. I have used Ennis Rees' translation, (New York: Random House, 1960) 34,63.

[6] G. S. Kirk and J. E. Raven, *The Presocratic Philosophers* (Cambridge: Cambridge University Press, 1975), pp . 94-96.

[7] Dio Chrysostom, *Orations*, no. 12.

[8] Sophocles, *Antigone*, 332.

[9] Homer, *The Odyssey*, Bk 5. Rees' transl. pp. 87-91.

[10] Homer, *The Iliad*, ch. 6, 208; Ch. 11, 783.

[11] See Preston H. Epps, *Thoughts from the Greeks* (Columbia, Missouri: University of Missouri Press, 1969) 121 - 130. I am greatly indebted to this small but delightful book for inspiration and ideas.

[12] Kirk and Raven, *The Presocratic Philosophers*, op.cit., 210.

[13] Clement of Alexandria, *Paidogogos*, Bk 3.1.

[14] Cf. K. W. Gransder, "Homer and the Epic" in *The Legacy of Greece*, ed. by M. I. Finley (New York: Oxford University Press,

1981) 111.

[15] Plato, *Theaitetos*, 174

[16] Ibid., 176a-c.

[17] Clement of Alexandria, *Paidagogos,* Bk 3.1.

[18] Deacon Agapetos, *Paraenesis,* sec. 3.

[19] Epps, op.cit., pp. 14-25.

[20] Plato, *Phaedo,* 1 1 5e.

[21] Plato, *Crito,* esp. 3-7. Loeb Classical Library edition (Cambridge, Mass., 1966) 154-63.

[22] Homer, *The Iliad,* Bk 2.210-75.

[23] Hesiod, *Works and Days,* esp. 290-380.

[24] Plutarch, *Solon,* ch. 14, cf. ch. 16.

[25] Ibid. ch. 27.

[26] Aristotle, *Politics,* 1265b (11.6.12); 1320a (VI.3.4).

[27] See chapters 6 to 12 of *Greece and the Hellenistic World,* ed. by John Boardman, Jasper Griffin and Oswyn Murray (New York: Oxford University Press, 1988) and especially J. C. Stobart, *The Glory that Was Greece* 4th edition edited and revised by R. J. Hopper (New York: Praeger Publishers, 1971) 128-81.

[28] See Bernard W. W. Knox, *Oedipus at Thebes,* p. 11.

[29] Euripides, *Fragments,* no. 910.

[30] Plato, *Laws,* 716c.

[31] Edgar M. Krentz "Roman Hellenism and Paul's Gospel" *The Bible Today* 26 (November 1988) 328-37, esp. 334.

[32] See my *Byzantine Philanthropy and Social Welfare,* 2nd revised and enlarged edition (New Rochelle: Aristide D. Caratzas, Publisher, 1991), ch. 1.

[33] Aeschylos, *Prometheus Bound,* pp. 28-30.

[34] Plato, *Laws,* iv. 713d.

[35] Xenophon, *Memorabilia* , IV.3. 3-7.

[36] Plato, *Symposium,* 1 99D, 301d; for a full discussion see Epps, pp. 65-85; Bruno Snell, op.cit., p. 273.

[37] Kathleen Freeman, *Ancilla to the Pre-Socratic Philosophers* (Cambridge, Mass.: Harvard University Press, 1978) 43-44.

[38] Kirk and Raven, *Presocratic Philosophers,* op.cit., pp. 400-26.

[39] Hippocrates, "The Oath," in *Hippocrates with an English translation,* Loeb Classical Library, 4 vols.

[40] Cited by Adolph Harnack, *The Mission and Expansion of Christianity,* vol. 1, p. 128.

[41] See Boardman, Griffin, Murray, *Greece and the Hellenistic World,* op.cit., pp. 368-79.

[42] Homer, The *Iliad,* Bk 24, 527.

[43] Cited by George Long, *The Meditations of Marcus Aurelius* (London, n. d.) 90.

[44] See Hans-Georg Gadamer, *The Idea of the Good in Platonic-Aristotelian Philosophy* (New Haven, Conn.: Yale University Press,

1986).

[45] Werner Jaeger, *Paideia: The Ideals of Greek Culture,* tr. by Gilbert Highet, 3 vols (Oxford: Basil Blackwell, 1946), vol 1, p. xiii.

[46] Ibid. p. xvii.

[47] Menander, *Fragments,* no. 761.

[48] Diogenes Laertios, *Lives of Eminent Philosophers,* Bk ii ch.11, 115. Edited with an English translation by R. D. Hicks 2 vols. (Cambridge, Mass.: Harvard University Press, 1959), vol. 1, pp. 242-44.

[49] Raymond E. Brown, *The Gospel According to John I-XII* (New York, 1966) 18.

[50] Harry Fournier, *Konstantinos Broumides* (Athens, 1980); Josephine G. Tighe, "Brumidi-Michael Angelo of the Capitol," *Fine Arts Journal* (Chicago, 1910), 106.

[51] Sophocles, *Oedipus at Colonus,* 54c.

[52] Plotinos, *On the Three Primary Hypostases,* Vl, k4. 10-11.

[53] Simplikios, *Commentary on Epicteti Enchiridion,* 5, 4-11.

[54] For example see the prayers of the Blessing of the Waters for Theophany, *Ieratikon,* (Athens: *Ekdosis Apostolikes Diakonias,* 1977), pp. 251-55. For an English see translation Joseph Raya and Jose de Vinck, *Byzantine Daily Worship* (Allendale, N. J.: Alleluia Press, 1968), pp. 597-604.

[55] Allan Bloom, *The Closing of the American Mind* (New York, 1987), p. 381.

[56] J. C. Stobart, *The Glory That Was Greece,* op.cit., pp.

[57] Arnold Toynbee, *The Greeks and Their Heritages* (New York: Oxford University Press, 1981), p. viii.

Index of Names

Printed in the United States
26304LVS00001B/244-267